Dancing, with Mirrors

# Dancing, with Mirrors

*George Amabile*

The Porcupine's Quill

Library and Archives Canada Cataloguing in Publication

Amabile, George, 1936–
    Dancing, with mirrors / George Amabile.

Poems.
ISBN 978-0-88984-343-1

    I. Title

PS8551.M32D35 2011        C811'.54        C2011-906070-1

1    2    3    ·    13    12    11

Published by The Porcupine's Quill, 68 Main Street, PO Box 160,
Erin, Ontario NOB 1TO. http://porcupinesquill.ca

Readied for the press by Wayne Clifford.

Represented in Canada by the Literary Press Group.
Trade orders are available from University of Toronto Press.

We acknowledge the support of the Ontario Arts Council and the Canada
Council for the Arts for our publishing program. The financial support of the
Government of Canada through the Canada Book Fund is also gratefully
acknowledged. Thanks, also, to the Government of Ontario through the
Ontario Media Development Corporation's Ontario Book Initiative.

Canada

Ontario
Ontario Media Development
Corporation

Canada Council    Conseil des Arts
for the Arts      du Canada

ONTARIO ARTS COUNCIL
CONSEIL DES ARTS DE L'ONTARIO

For my partner, Annette
and our son, Evan

# Contents

Invisible
skirmishes kick up dust and skid across the river
mirror:

stillness turns
back on itself

releasing
these fragmentary histories,
a shadow dance

between what happens in the world
and what goes on
inside.

# Tangents & Vectors

### 1

Hundreds of white stars
on the windshield.

Dawn is a salmon run
of tail lights. Exhaust
curdled by the arctic
weather churns
in place, the air

so tight
if feels unsafe to breathe.

### 2

Plastic
tacked up against the chill
                              slurs
faces crossing the sky-walk.

### 3

Freezing rain
smeared across the windshield
like a bird's eyelid
changes the carbon street lights
to chartreuse and purple
flares from deep space.

4

The law is all
        that's left of good
                intentions.
We pass it copiously like roe.
But there is no
        such thing
as a closed system.
Even our cells are free to defy their codes
and locked-up toxins crawl back
                    through rock
into earth, water, air.


5

In the tight box
of the skull, the brain
crackles with electric
perceptors; steel
           corridors
of the cyclotron hum;
each magnum
energy burst lights
           a brief
history of time
           but why
should it matter
that molecules from the first star
survive in the blood
of a rapist if they fail
to correct his behaviour?

6

I step out
into the sheer daze

of summer, looking
to make friends, love

or a killing.
Direction

is an accident.
Save me one dance.


7

Daylight
blackens the leaves.

Crows in the city.
Thunder and white rain.

Tires peel a slick, misty
tape away from the street.

Sails in the bay.
A tilt field

of Japanese paper.
When she laughs like that

deep in her throat
it sounds like water.

8

She tells me love is eternal
marmalade, a sacred mush
flecked with significant bitters.

After the last late show
The national anthem
roars like an empty cage.


9

Sometimes history changes key and soars.
Sometimes it sits there like a damaged animal.

At night, cliques of private light
scurry over the river.


10

The purity of absence
kindles appetites that hiss
and fuse. One
last beginning. A thought
hardens and sinks
into sea light. Labs
and museums. The mind
accelerates around its jar
of immortal embryos.

11

Altar. Bank.
Standard of living.
Rumours. Contracts. War.

# Burnt Wings

### 1

Chicken fat sizzles on propane barbecues.
The river shoulders its huge
                              indifference
through miles of crumbling
earth. It's not the world
I loved as a boy, with one leg
in that red wagon, pushing
hard, faster
and faster until the ball of my foot just
grazed the cement, flying
                              into the great white sun
where I would shout
my unrepeatable name and explode.


### 2

Approaching escape
velocity I came down
with a case of viral pneumonia.

The priest made a rare house call
with his book, his candles
and his fair, weathered face.

After the rapid syllables
hummed in a monotone
over the simmer of bean soup from the kitchen

there was the old silence, harmless
and without degrees. Profit
continued to drive a wartime economy.

3

I lay on a daybed in the darkened living room
feeling my thighs melt from their bones.

A horde of minute barbarians ate my lungs.
I tried to eat them back. No luck.

So I slipped away into soft kingdoms.
Centuries later, sparrows

quarrelled in fresh leaves and sunlight
glowed through the stained window shade.

It looked like an antique parchment
map of the New World.


4

Thistles don't care.

When I staggered into the brisk light
of May, they
                were prickly and stubborn.
                Lilacs were nearly the same
                colour but they
                                were kind.

        The wind played with my hair
        then pushed me over.

I got back up. I dreamed
there were no animals left
in the city. Even the rats
had climbed at night
on hawsers over a slack tide
onto the last freighters.

I took to lounging on the porch
with *The Hunchback of Notre Dame.*

Clouds went by.
The neighbourhood drunk
sang me a song about Garibaldi.
It felt as though thin bandages
had come loose
                    and sailed
away from his broken heart.

Lilacs bloomed in the dooryard.
My mother smiled like blue milk in my dreams.

5

Strength returned
just in the nick of time.
I learned how to stand
by. My heart grew happy
to spend whatever was left
of its time in a nest of rules.

6

Geometry seduced me.
I loved its desert of abstract events,
the invisible points, the lines,
the axioms.
                    Sea-wrack
seduced me too, sun
warming old wood, old shells,
the slow reach and retreat of the tides,
the rainbow mist
blown up over the rocks
by the waves, the wet
streets, the cobblestones and weeds.


7

*I've been walking all day, barefoot*
*down a dusty road. I don't know why*
*I'm here or where I'm going.*
*I push on through sunset into the dark.*
*Flowers close all around me.*
*When the moon appears, it looks drawn,*
*exhausted. Up ahead, where the road*
*curves, I see him, dancing,*
*a silly man in the white suit of a clown.*
*Red, blue and yellow stars*
*pulse from the cloth*
*and drift off into the forest.*
*He takes my hand.*
*We leave the road, laughing,*
*skipping through dead leaves.*
*They whisper comforting news*
*about the night that cannot surprise us,*

*and suddenly we are cosmic*
*acrobats, leaping*
*from one galactic fingerprint to the next,*
*higher and higher until I see*
*that his eyes are white*
*as ice when he smiles*
*and his teeth are set*
*in rows like the teeth of a shark.*


8


To him it was just a swat, a quick
spank on a diapered butt.
                              To the child, lifted
by one arm into the air, surrounded
by all that anger it was terror, and he
screams, not with pain, but with the shock
of knowing flight is impossible, of being
too weak, too small to fight back.

In time the shame
of that humiliation turns to venom.

The father cannot fathom
how he has changed
from partner, mentor, friend
to a predator that stalks the boy in his dreams.

9

In the empty Safeway parking lot
after a stormy night,
in a black

    depression filled with rain

        a film of oil changes the drab light
        to streaks and patches – fluorescent
        yellow, magenta, peacock blue,

          then the painful fiesta

            of dawn begins, and it's clear:
            I am a part of the morning,
            the part that watches while it burns.

# What We Take with Us, Going Away

1

All morning, beginning
with false dawn, darkness
recedes,
        dissolves,
                but is never entirely absent
from the rustle of unhurried light
in the trees, from the shimmer of heat waves,
from the flecked textures of cliff and rock.

All afternoon, clouds
                catch
and colour the sunlight
while their shadows dab
jaguar patches on the sea.

And now there's something new
in the air, a softening
                of edges,
the first shades of night, disguised
as a mood shift, *presto* to *andante*.

After a while there's this
                tug, as though
the undertow of something
I know but have forgotten
is trying to open the closed book of the past,
not in memory, exactly, but just
                under
whatever I see,
        as Puerto Escondido
fills with that nameless longing
I felt as a child alone on the street,
or standing in wet sand, watching
lights come on across the water.

2

It's darker now, but there's some light
left between clouds,
and a faint rim of gold on the horizon.

I hear someone singing. It drifts up from the shadows
that cluster around a lick of tangerine flame
on the beach. Other voices enter the song
and mix
        with the chirr
of crickets from a dozen summers.

The breeze is tannic with woodsmoke.
As it builds to a long rush in the trees
I can almost remember, that desire
for a stab of light at the edge of the sky,
for thunder, and rain, but it's gone
like a melted taste before I can place it,
and in that moment – as though darkness
had brought into focus what was there
but nearly invisible all day – I see the deep
-sea shrimper out in the bay.
The steering house and its three spars
are crusted with lights like a crown
and this time the memories wrestle free –
a Yugoslavian freighter, the *Hrvatska*,
thirteen days out of New York
to Algeciras, Tangiers, Genoa –
a loose constellation
adrift on the darkening waves,
almost empty, almost everyone gone
ashore, but it burns and rocks in the night wind,
a starred place, a sprung lock of returns and departures.

3

My mother has that look, the one
that tells me she does not expect,
or even hope for the life she imagined
for me before I was born.
We are near
                -ly strangers,
but she has come a long way
to see us
                off, on this tumbledown dock,
in the city of her birth.

When she holds me, then my wife,
and the child of our
                        unhappiness, briefly
in her arms, in her strong arms,
I know she is thinking about my father,
how love can change
to a not-so-simple politics
of need. She chooses her words
firmly. 'You don't really see
how quickly time passes when you're young.
Be good to each other ...'

4

I prop my elbows on the rail, inhale
fresh paint, diesel oil, brackish water, creosote
and fish. The salt wind combs my hair. Steadily
we move away from all that was once
familiar. It looks exotic now,
though I recognize that thin strip of sand,
South Beach, where I lost
myself in those eternal summers
watching the big, seagoing ships
grow smaller and smaller until they blinked
into a distance I could barely imagine.
I promised myself someday I'd be on one.

I should feel the arc of that desire
close. Instead, I remember my father
who made this crossing to the Great War
and back to his life before me. I see him, wedged
into a desk at the back of a roomful of children,
taking grade seven, grade eight.
Like so much else about him I learned this
from others. He never spoke to me
directly, except about saws, axes, hammers
and nails; he believed children belonged
to the distant and irrational world
of women, believed it so well
he couldn't say my name, but called me
                              Jo-Jo,
a diminutive
            of my mother, Josephine.

I'm wearing his ring, the one he kept
in the safe. It was a gift
from his mother, the day he became
a civil engineer. The white gold
engraved with leaves and flowers,
the large diamond, the nearly black amethysts,
were too rich for his Spartan reticence.
What I like best is the fact that he never wore it.


    5


We set up a playpen on deck. Natasha crawls
to the net fence at the edge of her world
within worlds
and stands up, dances, her hands over her head,
her already musical voice addressing

                       monologues
to the wind
        off the sea, to the gulls, dolphins, whales.

6

He would have loved this child. I can see him
flushed from his eternal work
in the yard, guzzling orange juice,
his shirt drenched with sweat, how he turned
suddenly shy in her presence,
how he tried to be chatty but failed.
Then, without warning,
she took his clumsy, calloused hand
and placed it so he could feel
the soft kick and swirl
of his grandchild.
                    He looked at me then,
through a small gleam
of triumph. Now you'll find out was all he said,
but under his cryptic omniscience
I sensed a change, a beginning.
                    She was born
thirty-one days after he died, dozing
in a rocking chair, watching the fights on TV.

7

Someone has handed me a white
carnation. Its fragrance
invades me and I throw it, hard,
at the grave, and when I turn
to leave I'm closed
in, by shocked faces, angry stares.

Short, bald, very deaf and almost
ninety, Tony 'elephant ears' waves
it off, his big voice patching
the rift. 'The boy
gives no disrespect. It's grief, *his* grief ...'

His arm is a hook
of muscled steel at my waist.
He guides me back to the limo.
'You come to us, now,' he growls,
'anytime.' I smile, nod
yes, though we know
I'll never see him again.

8

The ship's doctor leans back
in his deck chair, a shaggy-headed Russian
alcoholic. He is playing

chess with a twelve-year-old
from Zagreb. The boy is intense,
but patient. I watch them for hours,

over the edge of a book
by Turgenev. It's almost magical,
the way the doctor changes

classical patterns just enough
to force the child beyond them,
and the child responds, eager

but also thoughtfully
cautious, working it out.
They don't talk much, but smile

when they see patterns lock,
or dissolve. Day
after day, they take the game

to stalemate.

9

I remember a photograph,
the only one I've ever seen,
in which my father looks happy,

his arm hung loosely, easily
over my shoulders in the forgotten sun.
But that was before

the accident that killed
my brother, and the trial
where he stood at the back

of the courtroom in his trim
fedora, his suit and vest and gold
watch chain while I raised

my hand and swore
to tell the truth which he taught me
was always the right thing

to do, no exceptions.
The man who drove the truck
went free. My honesty

had betrayed us.

10

Four days at sea. She is not happy. Cold
bottles of vodka, free, instead of wine with lunch,
with dinner. I'm half drunk all the time now,
and I wonder, what did I hope
                              to discover
by living
          in Rome until spring
uproots us
          again? The sheer
extravagance of it all overwhelms me,
spending his money
in ways that would make him writhe
in the dirt. Maybe that's
what it means, this dizzy rise,
this nauseating shift
                        and drop
among the mountainous, gold-laced waves,
endlessly, across the Atlantic,
but I'm no longer sure of what I feel
when I lie all afternoon
                          in the lower bunk,
or wake just before dawn
to stand at the bucking rail, watching
stars fade to grey at the edge of the world.

Party tonight, our last
bash before landfall. I drink alone
in the stateroom, listening
to baby snores and watching the rats,
fat as kittens and nearly as tame,
climb the pipes, the cables,
and scurry across the top of the thin
partition. Hours of this.
I doze, and wake to the thud
of bodies fumbling against the door,
a wet kiss and a sigh.

As she enters the dark
                                room
her silhouette pulses with light.

She wants to make love. There's the usual
question. Her answer is breathless
and rushed. 'It's okay,
I put it in, just in case.' I'm tense
at first, but she whispers, 'Relax,
nothing happened,' and it's the best
sex we've had for months, for years.

12

I wake before dawn feeling sick.
Blinded
by the sudden light of the head,
I root around in the toiletry bag
for aspirin, for Dramamine, and the square, pink
plastic case escapes, hits the floor, pops
its catch and there
it is, a fat
white lie dusted with talcum.

13

Tangiers. Neat
                as a movie set,
dazzling stucco and the cut
                        shade
of red-and-white-striped
awnings in the tight, scrubbed streets.
Even the Casbah,
fragrant for once with incense and flowers,
is clean as it gets for the king's visit.

He won't notice
the man bundled in grey gauze
crouched at a stall the size of a closet
selling chunks of coal by the ounce,
or the beggar wrapped in a shawl of flies.

In this tiny historical moment
of preparedness and expectation,
reality
        shocks me.

I could be a father again come spring.

14

Genoa. Natasha sleeps in the second bed.
We sit near the window, playing
chess by candlelight.
The breeze is rich with harbour smells.
Voices come up from the street.
The lights of bars and restaurants
blink through the haze.

Her face is serenely beautiful
in the shadows, and it's clear
she has more courage, more faith
in this earth and its future than I do.

15

Over the edge of a picture book
                    about Switzerland,
I watch her lean against the train window,
amused, by the way Natasha rides
her hip, and waves, at crags
                    and shadows,
the stately gestures of rock face and cloud.

As the tracks curve, a rift
                    opens
its huge stone gates, disclosing
meadows, red roofs, the smoke
rising, a page out of *Heidi* ...

When the child turns, and stares
to catch my attention,
*a formidable natural border*
shrinks to bits of melting ice
in eyes blue as the Marjelensee.

16

Thessaloníki. In the twelfth century
monks ascended
                    the huge stone pillars
carved by a prehistoric river
and walled themselves in.

Plague fires burned in the body dumps.
The only smoke that reached them smelled of wax.

Today the one they've left as a guide
with egg in his beard and a rash
under the hair at the back of his neck tells her, 'No
the female animals go …'
into his ark of masculine darkness.

Under smoke-blackened roof beams
by faltering altar light, bits of broken tile
compose the gilt-haloed faces of saints.
Drained by history's meaningless pain
they look up to heaven and weep.

As he leads me through the cramped vestry
I notice how the skewed window
frames her abstracted figure, warped
by dimpled glass, her thighs
braced against a waist-high wall,
the wind in her hair, listening
to the music of goat-bells
and water running under the snow.

17

Tivoli, the Villa Adriana

The fountains glistened with sound as the wind rose.
Hadrian watched a water-jet struggle to keep
its willowy presence firm in a storm of rainbows
and saw Aphrodite, crowned with foam, deep

in the mind.
            Ruins.
                    How many shrines, stars,
empires have fallen since then? A second wind
sweeps the reflective pool to chipped marble
and seems to buffet the caryatids who stand

around, on edge, waiting, the soaked cloth
of their garments pressed flat against thigh and nipple
by imagined weather, by desire *eased out of thought*
and found again under the powdering tip

of a chisel. It blows where I stand now, *has* blown
for thousands of years, in the flesh, between water and stone.

I walk the dark streets
of Rome for hours, climb
stone stairs toward a window
that soaks clotheslines
and laundry with kitchen light,
cross a piazza, follow a crumbling wall
back toward the heart
of the city and come out,
blinking, into the glare
of the American Bar.

The place is almost
empty. A woman
sits by herself. Light
from the shape-shifting flame
of a candle plays
over her face, her full body
tunic the colour of olive
leaves, and makes her look
like a reflection on water.

I can almost see
piano notes like drops of rain
startling jewels and circles
from the cut flow
of oak in her tabletop.

I watch a current of blue
smoke speed up and slip
through an air vent's crusted grid
*like the ghost of a river*
*lost in a city of dust.*

19

She's not interested. She says it's because I go out
too much. Tonight she's not even
polite so I go out
                        again, but it's too late
for the Luau or the American Bar and I drive
north, to a place I know near Viterbo,
an all-night café that has the charm
of a psychiatric ward, blank walls, fluorescence,
the barman in a white jacket, Formica tables
and chrome chairs that skreak on the tiles.

By the time I arrive it's filled with smoke
and a band
                of gypsies. Desperate
                                for company,
I talk for hours in broken Italian,
but after five cappuccinos I need to get back
on the road. At first I'm distracted,
                                then hypnotized
by a spotlight that bounces and weaves,
                                veers
into my lane. I steer
left but the motorbike
driver jerks
            awake,
tries to get back on the right. Brakes
shriek, but it's too late; his young, shocked face,
his heavy, T-shirted shoulders
rise and there's a
sickening thud
when his head hammers the roof, just above
the suddenly spiderwebbed windshield.

I step out onto the pavement.
Smoke boils in the headlights.
He's lying on his back,
arms crossed over his chest.
My mind spins …

                    It was late
morning. Woodflies
whirled around our heads. I struggled
with his hand-me-down bike, the bent
frame, the loose chain
I cut my knuckles fixing; I shouted, S T A Y
B E H I N D  M E every time
he stood on the pedals, tall
in the saddle of my new Schwinn,
trying to surge by his big brother.

I heard the rattle of a dump truck, a screech
of brakes, then the gunshot
of a burst tire. Over my shoulder,
a splitsecond glimpse of handlebars
raking the air at a sick angle,
milky smoke and a black
smear on the highway. I was in the air
when his body slammed on the grass
shoulder, rolled up in a heap.
I landed running, tearing
                          his name loose
from my throat.
                I knelt, still
shouting, trying to shake him
awake, then rocked him senseless in my lap.

I kneel now, in broken glass,
in the headlights of stopped traffic, feeling
his cold neck for a pulse, confused
by the scent
              of wine
in the air, and my breath
                          explodes
when I understand,
                    he's dead
drunk, and snoring.


                    20


She doesn't trust the doctors,
can't speak a word
                    of Italian.

We agree that she should have the child
with her mom, in Arkansas.
But I'm not ready to let go
of Europe.
            At the airport
we kiss half-heartedly
and I drive back to pack for my trip.

A friend, the poet Robert Bagg,
puts it all in perspective,
'Now it begins, the old war
between loneliness and freedom.'

21

Baiano. My mother's people lived here
for centuries, for millennia, even before
the Roman aristocracy built villas
and cured their aches at the sulphur springs.

Hardly anyone visits now. A few old men
in black hats doze on a bench in the piazza.
The day is measured by wind
in the chestnut trees, by church bells
and the chittering drone of cicadas.

'*Masi?*' He nods. '*Ah, si,
molti anni fa, tutti sono andati via.*'


22

My great-grandfather's house
is a stone shell,
                without window glass,
with no doors
                in the doorways.

But the wine is cheap and has the fragrance of flowers.

23

Positano. I try to write,
but the past keeps closing.

Through the long afternoons
I walk the terraced hills
and slowly, in the company
of olive trees that have survived
for centuries in the twisting wind,
I open myself to the helplessness,
the guilt of my brother's death.

24

How could such a thing happen?
Is anyone to blame?

I let him ride my Schwinn
but why did I think he'd stay
behind me, when, for him,
it was just another game
he'd do his best to win?
I should have known he'd try
to overtake me again
with an all-out burst
of speed when we reached the highway.
I should have let him go first.

They said it didn't matter,
by the time I reached him he
was already past help
but I've never been able to answer
the question I've asked myself
a thousand times: Why
did I try to wake him up?
I should have just let him lie there
but I couldn't. I shook him, I
rocked him to death in my lap.

My mother – who let herself be
talked out of her fear
and believed, too easily,
that my father as engineer
for roads like the Interstate
was right, if the sky was clear
it was perfectly safe to drive
our bikes on the grass beside
the highway – never forgave

herself;
       and my father – I
had never seen him falter
but I heard his clenched voice tear
as he cursed God that day
at his workbench, his altar
where he took himself to pray;

the driver, slouched and broken,
hugged me close to his chest
when I ran up and tried to choke him,
and yes, there was beer on his breath;

the neighbour who thought it was just
good business to hand out steaks
and whisky to keep that truck
on the road with bad brakes;
those who signed the forms
or looked the other way
believing it only normal
to bend the law for pay;

and my brother, well on his way
to a clear pass, his wheels
firm on the concrete pavement,
stair-stepping the pedals
of a sleek, new bike,
with nothing in mind but the knife-
edge of that moment,
wind in his hair, in his face,
and every nerve awake
to the last joy of his life …

## 25

I summon the glazed eyes
of my father, I try to say
what I felt that day at his grave,
'You were never there, and now
you've done it again, gone away
into impossible distance.
I really thought you'd see
that I told the truth in court.
I thought you'd be proud of me
but grief had dragged your heart
down to where human darkness
needs to explode the sun.
All you could think of, then,
was loyalty and vengeance,
the old codes of our blood.

'I remember the night you slapped me
when I asked you to step outside.
I waited there in the cold,
listening, while your voice
shook the house and my mother
pleaded. I needed to fight you,
to be done one way or another
with all that guilt, that fear.

'I'm sorry you stayed inside.
But let me ask you a question?
Were you ever satisfied
with the compromise you made,
out of love, or just maybe
because you were afraid
of the rage snaking inside you?'

His eyes flutter, he starts
to speak, but the withered folds
at his throat are a clutch
                    of roots.
His voice flakes off in the wind.


26


Paris. The Rodin Museum,
a small park, green
as the sea spotted with whitecaps
(his alabaster statuettes, so
smooth-skinned they seem
to have ripened here, in the shade
of leaves, their yin
and yang perfectly matched,
closed in the mysteries of Eros).


27


At the Saint-Germain apartment
of a man with a once-famous name
who makes an adventurous living
dubbing French movies,
we're having drinks, debating
the Politics of Art,
when a telegram finds me.
*Tamara Lee, born April 3rd,*
*awaits her father's arrival.*

28

Flying back to New York
after the stark beauty of Iceland
I wish I didn't have to
come down from the sky
and re-enter what looks like
a brownish, calcified eruption
spread for hundreds of miles
over the skin of the planet.


29

She lifts the infant from the crib
so easily, and holds her out to me.
Auburn hair like mine as a boy,
and eyes that have their silence
*somewhere I have never travelled.*

They say what I think they'll say
for the rest of our lives.
'I'm glad you're here, Dad,
but where the hell were you?'

*As far away from you, child,*
*as my father was from me.*

But when I take her,
and her strong body squirms
in my arms, it feels
as though I've just awakened from a dream.

I watch the shrimp boat steam out of the bay
like a cluster of stars
                that sinks
and blinks out at the edge of the world.

Crickets are taking the night apart
with glassy ratchets.

In the reef of lights across the *bahía,*
only the beacon has a pulse,
a small flare that insists,
*I am here. You are there.*

It's past midnight but the sun still burns
my skin, drawing out water and salt.
The sea explodes in a brace of rocks.

On the coast road, headlights
like tiny pairs of eyes,
flicker as they pass under sparse trees.

Back in the hills a storm
                shimmers.
Below, in the dark,
released by scruffy undergrowth,
green sparks drift,
             and melt.

*Fireflies.*

Above them, a meteor scratches the sky
and fades, leaving no scar, no trace
of absence, even, on the night's bright face.

31

When I first came to Oaxaca
I wandered for weeks
among the ruins of Uxmal and Chichén Itzá.
I climbed the Pyramid of the Sun,
took shelter from a thunderstorm
in the small stone room
where priests communed with savage gods
before their obsidian blades
sawed the hearts from thousands of captives.

But it wasn't their practice
of feeding human blood to the sun
that surprised me. (How many lives
do we sacrifice, every day, to machines
with names like Jaguar and Barracuda?)
What eluded me was how
they exchanged complex information
that let them construct and maintain
more than fifty sacred cities, webbed
in a single vision, but scattered
over two hundred thousand square miles.

I stood there looking out
through a frame of hewn stone,
at the bountiful rage of Tlaloc.
White strokes battered the leaves,
the paved causeways, the dome
with its vertical cuff and slit
exactly like Mount Palomar
where an ancient patience mapped the stars.
How did they manage all this
without computers, lasers,
fibre optics, telephone lines or the wheel?

It was the runners
coursing through jungle trails,
fuelled by small water skins
and twists of dried meat,
their nearly naked bodies
filmed with sweat, glistening
in sunlight and in the light of the moon.
They did not rest
or sleep for hundreds of miles
and no one cheered from the sidelines.

This is what I've learned
                    to admire:
how they unravelled the skein
                              of Fate
by putting one foot after the other
for years, for decades,
until they became one with the dust.

# Bachelor Suite

1

On the corner,
two little girls punch
a tetherball: bunched
papers in a plastic bag
tied with binder twine to the top
of a stop sign. Above them
the sunset burns, rose
then magenta, changing the pulse
of the city. A few cars
ease through the briefly magical
afterlight with a sound like forced
air and the spritz
of tires on leftover sand.

Another cold spring
evening turns into night,
and it comes again, the whole
past, absent-minded love, a child
at an open window looking down
out of his loneliness
into the street, into his life
to come, which is already more
than half gone, and thousands
of miles away it's me, looking out
through the husky silence,
thinking of home, wondering
what it was and how it has kept
such distant memories wet
with feeling, like a set
of slides, in a box
in the small back room
off the kitchen all these years.

2

I have new tools now, new skills,
but decisions are still edged
with risk. I plug in the chrome kettle
and see myself as I really am, big-headed
with pygmy arms and legs, the rest
of the world shrunk very small
and packed into the curved space behind me.

I know it's time to change
my underwear, my behaviour,
before tomorrow changes
into today, and today
fills with the rose light of nostalgia.

The water boils.
The sky is full of clouds.


3

Invention is the mother of necessity.
The more new things we make and learn
to depend on, the more time we have
to spend indentured to their service.
Sometimes I feel the need to resist,
even if all I can think of to do is lie
in bed, or on a grassy slope in the park,
all day, letting my mind fill to the brim
with air. I won't read a book
or listen to music. I won't make a call
or answer my cell. I won't even walk
to the store till the weekend's over.

4

On the desk,
in a tall earthenware mug,
a steel ruler
completely hemmed in
by a crowd of pointless pencils.

*Whatever needs to organize*
*by dividing, or believes*
*that discrimination is a triumph*
*over chaos will fail*
*to entertain possibility . . .*

A small pair of scissors
looks as though it wants to grow
wings, to jab, and wade
on stick legs in some tropical estuary.

Even when we are not aware
of them, shadows
breathe, quietly, in the shallows.

5

I admired him, but not enough
to follow his moods all the way through
that knot of despair into hopeless courage,
brooding and spreading a tragic air

over the simplest pleasures.
Years after an early retirement
he appears on TV, disowns
his accomplishments. Greatness,

he says, cannot exist in a trivial age.
The interviewer presses, cheerfully
espousing the thin rationales
of celebrity. He shakes

his head but does not refute her.
She asks him to share the secret of
Success. 'Luck.' He smiles.
'And a blind persistence, but

we have no test, no standard
for genius, and we are left
worshipping wealth
and fame.' Silence.

She looks as though
she'd like to blow his cover,
but before she can say I know
you don't really mean that he growls

'If you really need to get down
on your knees, why not
submit
            to the gods who dance
inside you?'


6


The last echo of sunset
survives in the highlights
that flash from stainless cookware
and glasses fresh from the sink.

As the window darkens,
the ghostly, aging face
I've lived with and ignored
for years, comes clear
like something inevitable
rising at last from deep water.

I go for a walk along the river,
come back, read a book,
but the image will not leave.

Insight, it seems, always arrives
just in time to smile and turn out the light.

7

The window is open, the air is hot
and still. There is that smell
of dusty screens mixed with a trace
of lilacs, of canned tomato
soup, hamburger grease,
onions and cigarette smoke.

Birds make desultory music
and shadows edge across the lawn
of the Balmoral School for Girls.

I should be grateful for this
brief time in which I'm not caught up
with some obsessive chain
of command, or suffocated by the press
of events. But I feel restless
and vaguely irresponsible
as the day goes on
without me. What is it,
this need to be involved
in the rapid exchange of force
-ful but always inadequate,
always partially blind verdicts
as though each one could change
the world *by an inch or an ounce* ...

8

Daisies would be nice, here
in the cool extinction of daylight
among the dusty furniture from another
life, the stopped clock,
                    the staggered
profiles
        of stacked boxes
                    and books,

or a soft voice, children
crooning over mementoes,
a woman, a face ...
                    The raised window
holds a smoky haze against the first
stars, like an eye dimmed by years
of grief.
        Down on the street
a woman in a black coat leans
on her cane. The bus is late.
It is always late. She won't sit
on the bench, but sinks
into shadow as street lights blink
on, startling the sunset.

9

The world is a tissue of useful fictions.

The more belief remains the same,
the more it enslaves us.

Even so, in time I may learn
to seize my peevish discontent
and shake it. A glimpse, a glimmer,
a gasp of awe from the borderless fields
of childhood may tumble out
and surprise me,
                        with its fragrance,
with its resilient
                        frailty,
and I'll give up
this life, this addiction
that scans, and scans
the horizon for something to drown in.

10

I turn into the back lane behind the hotel
and aim myself at the dented, aluminum-skinned
door. Light from a buzzing fixture
glazes the wet cement, lays a gloss
over puddles, and glitters from the edge
of a broken glass. I've been here
before, two or three times
a week for years, made easy jokes, shot
eight-ball with hustlers and friends,
filled up my time, my life, watching
sports and old movies.

What else is there?
Well, there's the mind
with its prim, fragile containments,
the nerves blitzing with split
-second connections, dreams
of life on unusual planets,
the sudden decay of this
or that continuum, germs
that are good for you (acidophilus, wheat).
Rope. Ladders. I think
of that great writer, EH,
focusing his remarkable intelligence
on the twelve gauge between his knees.
He's been sick for years.
He's tired. He's had enough.

After the bars close
I stand in the street looking up

at the lit room, orange
burlap lampshade on a tall

gold stem, imagining
how it would feel to be home

-less, and the glow from the window,
the desk, the neat row of books

begins to deepen
as if with the sweetness of words

like *shelter* and *grace*
till wind comes up off the river

roughing my hair, numbing my face.
Then I climb the worn carpeted stairs

and let myself in
for what?

12

Beside the Yamaha, the lampshade
collects light from the dusty globe

and pours it over my hands
on the keys

like spilt milk, tarnished
by too many years in the same

life, a motif
               of descending minors.

# Transit in Absentia

1

The terraced hillside
            steps
                    off into haze,

and the brisk
*italics* of winter

trees. The day turns
colder. I want to be

      absolute

-ly stupid as this wind, these glazed
patches of stone in the park ...

2

On the airport bus,
ice-light makes me think

we're crossing the badlands
of an abandoned planet,

sun dogs
like matched trumpet notes,

low dunes, white
and sleek as quicklime, smoking

where the wind whets
their curved lips, and now,

out of nowhere, this
graveyard without a fence,

this extinct outpost
of stones – weathered

inscriptions half silted up
with alkali snow – glides

by, behind glass, like some
diorama in a space
                    museum.

3

Morning. It's as though the world has been reinvented
with molecular technology, and now, instead of the old
landscapes, flawed by decay and redundance,

we have their simulacra, scrubbed
and bright. I walk into hot light, untouched
by the splash of magenta and blood

-red from a trellis, the cut
shadow of scavenger wings on the sand.
The sea folds over itself. The wind

is tinctured with local scents and a man
with mahogany skin and the traces
of sleep around his eyes carries

a silver fish by the tail. As I watch him
walk so easily across the burning beach,
a mild sense of wonderment overtakes me.

I have seen this glimpse of otherness
before, in a brochure,
and I know that I've chosen exactly the right

escape. White fishing boats
with striped canopies
flare and melt in the distant glitter.

4

The hotel pool has been stormed
by a flock of black *sanates.*
Their long tails bob and spread like fans
as they bathe in the complex ripples
that lap the top step,
or hop across the paved apron,
their eyes like opals packed in soot,
their necks pressed against the dimpled stone,
graphite beaks working
to scrape up sips of reflected sky.

When I look again through my Pentax
they're gone.
          I photograph bougainvillea,
gaudy petals without fragrance, fluttering
like dyed paper in the breeze ...

5

Andirons with skins
of apricot suede, copper
tabletops, the blue haze
of tonic water in which a twist
of lemon rides cracked ice
like a flash of yellow wings
over the river. Stripped logs
have been varnished and stacked
around the glass dance-floor
aquarium with its fat
carp and indolent flora. Soon
the sun will decline
in favour of the disco crowd
who have already brought themselves out
in ones, and threes. A young man
handsome enough for a postcard
is speaking of politics in a rickety
accent. Yes, well, respect is a mere
pittance, easy to be extracted
from the inferiors with a little
violence. A young woman agrees.
Both her transparent plastic shoes
are filled with money. She's been working
the crowd to buy drinks for her friends
in the band. She explains
how it will be in the new age,
that curious mix of boredom and lustre.
She thinks it will be grand.

6

A fuzzy half moon hangs from the bruised night.
It looks as though it has become infected

with an as yet uncatalogued fungus, tenacious
as angel hair. It has lost its place

in the old stories – Astarte, Nanna,
Hsi Wang Mu, or the Mexican Trickster

Conejo – and must be content
with its role as pockmarked veteran

of obscure plagues and wars,
the unearthly darkness packed like grease

around a bearing
that won't hold up much longer.

7

And all the while they were imagining
soft landings, the night sky,
the moon a pearl among diamonds,
the empty sleeves
                    of the sea.

Later, they abandoned themselves
to ambivalent shade, breathing
shallow afternoons and closing the books
they had leafed through as a hedge against boredom.
It was enough to dream with half-closed eyes,
to speak in fragments, in a vernacular
conditioned by boutiques and cafés.

Pods ripen and fall.

They gather their towels and cups,
their headbands, their unread mail,
and that is all they have time for
under cliffs with their fossil records
lying carelessly open
as braille in the decaying light.

8

The big boat shudders and hums.
Light sparkles under a thin mist.

As the stern
                veers
                        and steadies,
blue hills drift away. The gulls
adjust. The air-vent grilles
quiver and blur, and the waves,
slate grey like the backs
of the birds, change
textures: chipped
stone like a primitive axe-head,
hammered lead,
burred steel or a cross-hatch
of loosely woven linen …

The breeze dies. The sea is a mirror
filled with nothing but time.

9

The cities are streaked with blue exhaust.
In the hills, people are starving.
It is impossible to tell the difference
between the police and the army;
they prowl the streets with the same black
batons and assault rifles.

But on the beaches, there you feel free.
Cabanas doze in the shadows of palms.
The food is wholesome and surprisingly
inexpensive. At night, in the outdoor cafés,
young men move discreetly among the tables
offering silver, opals, rare carvings,
perfumed cigarettes or the intimate
attentions of children. From here
you can take an aqua-plane
to three international airports.

10

The 747
at 60,000 feet
hardly seems to move
above the ice-berg drift
of cumulus, loses
more and more ground
in its race against the westering light,
and as night overtakes us, it stalls
altogether, a ghost
ship becalmed among alien stars.


11

Back on once-familiar ground,
*turning and turning* through acute
switchbacks, all sense
of direction fails
as the scissor-shift of ridges and peaks
dissolves to an existential
*nausée,* a confusion
about what it means to go
                              away
and what it means to return.

On the left, a shudder of trees.
The rest is untranslatable.

12

I join a gaggle of tourists
crossing the white waste

of a glacier. It's like walking
on packed snow until we arrive

at this crevasse, a shadowy
fracture that looks like an earthquake

made it, but instead of earth
there's this descent into jagged blue

-hearted ice. Our guide passes
around a Styrofoam bucket, filled

with chunks of the stuff. Melt
this in your mouth, he says,

it will add years to your life.
I shake my head and smile politely.

13

The travellers have returned,
their clothes only slightly soiled,
their gear intact. Their eyes are still
bright with what they have seen:
mountains clean as flint chips,
blown curtains of snow.

There is a lightness, an absence
in the way they move
through the strange rooms of the house,
picking up and replacing things
they are not really sure belong there,
their glances, their fingers
lingering distractedly over surfaces, textures ...

The close air is faintly scented
with memory, and the shifting light recalls
a web of associations
they never thought about before,
but lived
          in, a habitude, a style
that has become remote, and they
demur, bemused, enclosed by shadowy moods
they recognize but cannot enter.

They are happy to be back; they say
this though their words are thin,
reaching like intangible probes
into all that was once careless
                         and familiar,
until their voices are more secure,
exploring fresh timbres, surprising
in their unaccustomed
                         spaciousness,
and as a comfortable silence opens
between, then around them, they turn
from each other,
                         and lose themselves in the view.

# Power Failure

1

What if it all happens
as predicted, the icefields melt,
the waters rise and the grid
blacks out?
                    I consult the cards.
I read newspapers and books.
I open the deep sea-chest
of the mind.
                    Nothing
but emblems and persuasions.

2

The phone ripped into thick sleep
like a chainsaw. It was already
late, for almost everything.

Yesterday was a blur,
a headache, and it hurt
to think of tomorrow.

No one was left in the house.
It was afternoon. The room
was filled with shadows, flashes

of storm-light and faint thunder.
I got dressed, came out
into the grey city, wondering

who had phoned.
                    I walk until the rain
stops, drips from the awnings,

the windowsills, and lights
come on in the wet pavement.
An ideology of sorts, this

aimlessness among strangers
where there is nothing I need
to do, nothing to fix

or empty, and with no
reason to go
back I walk on.

3

What I've always thought of
                    as Freedom
may just be a way
                    of wasting more and more time:
these week-long tours
of local shops, bars, museums,
afternoons in the sun, evenings
on the terrace, watching
harbour lights and stars. Hours.
Learning to blow smoke rings,
memorizing the names
of tropical birds, trying to choose
between Pineapple-Orange and Five Alive.

Time goes by, like spilt milk, like blood
under the bridge.
                    War
breaks out, a TV sports event, interrupted
by high-tech rumours and lies. The markets
wobble, rally, dip and slide
sideways. The graphs are jagged
cordilleras of profit and loss. A record
-breaking baseball great (retired) goes on
trial for palming a woman's breast in a club.
There's another earthquake, a flood; a volcano
smokes and glows all night. The magazines
are featuring questionnaires: Is it really
love? Are you wearing the right clothes
for your ethnic profile? Do you suffer
from invisible stress, boredom, depression,

whimsical irrelevance or an undiagnosed loss
of momentum? Pills. Potions. Regimens.
An assembly line of triggers and lures
becomes the world in which we are free
to drift, to go with the flow, to follow
trends and gurus and presidents, the path
of least intelligence, but no matter
how quickly we change brands, and partners,
the cutting edge of day will correct our dreams.


4


Somewhere, starlight
        flickers

on the wind-roughened face
        of the sea,

like the scattered remains
        of original

                violence.

5

Night after night
we see them on TV,
children, their eyes buzzed
by flies, staring
back at us from the edge
of extinction.


6

The sky is white and the wind
is cold. It scatters leaves
across the dead grass, like shadows
blown from the dreams I've lived
in but can't remember. Everything
I believe, or think I might
know has come apart,
and being here feels just the same
as being nowhere at all.


7

When warmth goes out of the world,
time slows to the pace of a glacier.
Walking, and walking, inside
the snow, nothing changes and there is no
difference between the earth and the sky.

8

Stalactites of ribbed ice hang from the eaves.
A whisky jack sits on a branch, cowlicked
by the wind. I wonder if he can remember leaves
or the tall grass that's been cut, bundled and hayricked.

Out on the frozen river, fishermen stare
at their rigs: a line, a bell, a black hole.
The sound that bristles along each wind flare
is loose change dropped into a bowl.

Snowflakes flicker like scratched light from an old
film, until the ski trails disappear
in the blurred air and the last gleam of cold
sun gives way to the darkest night of the year.


9

Snow changes the parked cars
to burial mounds. I remember
a spare room off the kitchen
in a city long ago. A telephone rings.
And rings, but no one's there …

10

She pounded my door at four in the morning
because she had gotten pregnant
again and we were friends.
She wanted to make love,
                                violently;
she thought it would make her miscarry.
I told her it wouldn't work. What about
the father? He doesn't know,
he's gone. She stayed with me
until her parents found her.
A few weeks later, she bled
herself to death in a closet.

                *  *  *

'Come to New York,' he said,
'we'll write that book.' My first
day in the city, a friend calls
from Poughkeepsie: *It's Grandin.*
*They found him this morning,*
naked, an empty vial on the desk,
his head on his arms,
his arms crossed on the Smith Corona,
and all the plugs pulled in the brightening room.

                *  *  *

We called it the Raven's Nest, that loft
where he lived on the roof of a warehouse.
He had talked about it often enough,
how Blake was right, how everything
was upside down and inside out.
I think I know what he was thinking
when he jumped; he was rising; at the star-
burst of impact he'd be free.

11

The clock ticks off quick, metallic heartbeats.
I remember her eyes, my arm around his shoulders,
passionate talk, whisky straight through the night.

A train whistle pierces the room.
I put on my coat and walk out as far as the stone bridge.
The river is frozen. The moon
                   breaks
                           from tangled branches
and sails out into a sea of stars. What if our species
is destined for oblivion, like so many others, like the sun
itself? Dark thought in a dark time. Somewhere,
from one of the houses, a saxophone
explores the ancient labyrinth of grief.

Earth scents and a taste of sun in the chill.

*April is the cruellest month.*

The wet street is a blaze of silk
but it will snow again. And melt, and freeze
again before the first buds open. This
is where tendencies contend, rapture,
denial, initiatives, composure pierced
by splinters of ice-melt, the grand elliptical
orbit dripping with halo death and stone fever.

Forward. Life goes on. We know
this. But we don't
know where, though we think
and say that *on* is better. How did we
arrive at this consensus? Would we
walk ahead with such unexamined
confidence if we had a better grasp
of ring theory or the tentative
contracts that exist between opals
and moonlight? Destitute ambition
flickers, has a moment of recognition,
flares outrageously, then dies
like a hot wick in a draft. The parks
are empty. The city is dark. The country
has lost its political will and the planet
itself spins and spins, endlessly
beyond any question of memory or desire.

13

The moon's reflection breaks
into flaked highlights
on the chipped obsidian plate
of the lake. This
is what I came for,
this vacancy, this absent-hearted night.

Watching shadows
                    move as the flames move,
I drift into shallow sleep.

Suddenly,
           I'm awake. It's cold.
Wind comes in off the water,
digging through layers of ash,
fanning the coals to an incandescent rubble
like the stones of a city
                          that was not there
before and won't be again.

14

Perfectability recedes, a dream-tide
island of towers and lights,
into mythic distance, into nostalgia.
And there is this
                    ease, this elision,
gliding along abstract vectors
toward some understanding that may not arrive,
except as an afterthought, accepting
impermanence as the price we pay
to enter the limitless play of forms,
where curiosity survives ambition, and the heart
is a thorax of muted glory, an infinite yes.

Think of it: you may never be
fully possessed of your life
as it exists in the eyes of others,
or as it may appear
to emerge from the cold trails
and fragments that will survive you.

This knowledge is physical, a pulse
of shadow selves, and it is not new,
this rustle of meaning that cannot resolve
the past, this continuous
nova of minor extinctions, flicker
and sift, a veil or scrim, crackling
with scintillae that fades
into the spark-field of old constellations.

Desultory highlights forecast
flawed permutations we can't resist
or ignore, as the seasons, like huge sails,
adjust the thousand shades of desire
that have led us to this climate
in which all surfaces dissolve
and the wind goes on
refusing to tell us our names.

# First Light

1

Birdsong. A few scattered notes
that flare and melt in the dark,
even before the vague streets and parks
begin to invade the night's brief
                              amnesia.

Leafless trees, moth-eaten mats
of dead grass, cracks
in the street packed with snow, the first
bus bunting its blunt head through the hush,
and over the husk of St. Augustine's church,
the faint, nearly transparent moon
has a shocked face, like the ghost
of an infant ripped from its mother
                              's breast in a storm.


2

        Mystery gives way
to belief, and belief gives way
            to knowledge,
and the small teeth of the mind
            grind on, though safety
is nothing more than time disguised
            as a clock.

3

Perhaps our thoughts are nothing
but ghostly paradigms
of need, crushed
whenever they explore
unspeakable worlds that fade
with the dawn.
                          On the street
fistfuls of dusty noise
assail them. We invent
new theories but then we stop
to breathe and a glimpse
of everything at once dissolves
their sensitive connections.

Fog swirls in the park, erasing
the trees, the granite horsemen.


4

Steaming tea in a glass cup on the desk.
*Light is the Lion that comes down
to drink* … I admire those words, the risk
they take, like saying, 'My mind is grass, brown
or green in the sun of centuries, in Africa
where human life began …' and yet
they seem far-fetched. Morning traffic
crawls like a herd while sun dogs threaten
the body and the mind with such vivid cold
it's hard to see how the Cree, with their simple flames
and skins, could survive it. And what of the lion, sold
into sleep at the zoo? Is he the same
final consumer clothed in scruffy gold
who came to drink, and cleared the water hole?

5

*Humankind cannot bear very much*
*reality.*
　　　　Paint the windows
black. Disappear
behind complex deconstructions.

But a thin
　　　　　　edge, a crack
of sun under the door, angry
or magical, cuts
　　　　　　　　through layers of denial,
floods the inertia of theoretical space
with fresh consignments
　　　　　　　　　　and representations:
the flux
　　　　we inhabit
　　　　　　　that inhabits
　　　　　　　　　　us.

6

White gusts batter the window,
so thick I can't see the street.

In the pearl and opal glow
the snug room with its hewn beams,
the solid furniture,
even the bowl heaped with fruit
seem insubstantial, as though
the wind might slip
through them or blow them away.

I kneel before ticks and whispers,
the sudden rush of flame, the roar
that puffs a drift of soot from the flue.

Is it really the same
insatiable appetite that raised a storm
of sparks in the dream time,
the snow like a huge bird
beating its wings against the mouth
of the cave, scattering
embers and charred bones, driving us
back,
        into a choked throat
of stone, into darkness
and hunger, and broken sleep?

The grey crust cracks,
                    collapses;
the glare inside survives, breeds
crimped threads
                    of smoke that stretch
and vanish
            into a black absence
where something very old
howls
        and is still.

A backdraft floods the room
with harsh scents, with moments
the body almost remembers,
terror and wonder and grief
preserved, but inaccessible
as the unwritten history of fire and snow.

Flecks of nearly invisible shadow
swim over the floor, the furniture, my clothes, my skin,
like the first signs of life in a bleached sea.

7

In the beginning there was always
(though we left it like a shed
skin to dry at the back of the cave
of the mind) the need
                          to know
what went on before us.

Believing what we thought
we remembered, we began
to obey imperatives: Fate,
Gods, Biology, dream work, stories
about the star at the core
of an apple, the oracle
with her tossed bones,
the scrolls, the cards, the prophet
who returns from the desert with wild eyes.

To begin is always to enter again
days that have already come
to pass: visions eaten without salt
by fanatics; milestones, codes, epiphanies,
collapsed suns in the mind ...

When mayflies tumble
                    out of the sky
to litter the sidewalks and pavements
of lakeside resorts;
                    when comets
with tighter schedules than buses or trains
return from the limitless night
we lived in before we knew
how to scratch
                    pictures on the walls
of caves, insights
flash through a husk
of selves and the light
they admit reveals
as it fades
                    a shadow dance,
a slipped encounter soft as rain.

8

It's almost new, this metal
railing, wet after a hard
rain. I set my elbows
into cold sweat and look upriver.

    A breeze I can't feel yet fans out
    from its nesting place among fresh leaves
    thrumming a stretch of dull water
    raising a bright hatch like insect wings

and the first cars
begin to nose out of the side streets
their sealed beams brisk
and unnecessary
under the brightening sky
which has already washed
faint cloud shadows
over those the still-burning
street lights make
out of boughs, birds
and me
and there is this

    lightness

        as though the soft gates of the body
        had begun to exchange personal history
        with the drift of river time
        like the mix of matched guitars
        the raw voice of a blues harp
        words pulled out of memory muscle and sweat
        Kimberly's big eyes fluttering shut
        her slender legs curled in a sleeping bag

the delicate snore that flared her nostrils
almost in four-four time
like the crickets
like the rain that shook the windows
like the fridge in the kitchen
kicking in, like the embers
ticking, under a crust
of ash ...

On the river
tiny wings of light
                    dissolve
into a watercolor:
violet-edged skyline
dotted with bright green
impressionist trees.

        *My fingertips burn*

            *on the strings. The music*
            *starts again.* The wine
            got crisper as it chilled
            in its wash of melting ice
            then there was brandy
            and smoke wasting away
            in the air, its buzz
            already fading from the blood
            which cleans itself
            incessantly like a cat ...

        When I hit the street
        for the long walk back
        it was night. Now

it's morning. The bridge
trembles under my feet
as traffic rumbles over the Red
into a trapped stampede.

　… always

　　　after lots of nothing much
　　　there is this unpredictable
　　　rightness, like the breeze
　　　that starts again and blows
　　　the reflection
　　　of our urban renaissance
　　　apart like a puzzle
　　　only stillness has the heart
　　　to heal

　　　　and I can't tell
　　　　whether we sang better
　　　　on brandy or wine
　　　　or water cold from the tap

　　　　　and I don't know why I think

　　　　　　of Patrick in Swift Current
　　　　　　the stone he brought
　　　　　　home like a lost pet
　　　　　　and the stone's lichen
　　　　　　exactly the colour of glacial till
　　　　　　but white at the edges
　　　　　　like a drying lake
　　　　　　seen from the top of a mountain
　　　　　　the sprinkle of rain
　　　　　　he shook from his own hands
　　　　　　four times a year, and the way
　　　　　　he'd stand and observe it

patiently open-minded
as the sky

and yes, it's outrageous
to indulge in these
unprofitable pastimes
while the living
we should be making starves
and the banks

of the river fail,
crumbling
into little whirlpools

as the city smokes and breaks
new ground.

It's Monday but the moon is thin
a memory trace
over the brawling world.

## out of the cradle

rock is not the bottom.
there is no bottom.
there are no lines either.

there is the sea
*endlessly rocking*
stones
at the edge
of the mind. and there

are tiny survivors
the eye can't see
who split and go on
splitting. and the first
is also the last
because they're one
and the same.

2

Are we one,
or the same?
The mind says yes
but it doesn't feel
that way, it feels
as though this
me, this old skin,
this singularity
I've tried to shake
for decades won't
ever shrink
to the hub
of a web or explode
into the oversoul,
that spirit which is
everywhere
at once, no
it feels as though
there's only this
body and its
death which has
never happened
before, no matter
how many have gone there.

3

Between islands
where the riptide
turns, they kill
the engine, let
the boat
          drift,
                    and slip
the craft of millennia
into that now
                    alien
atmosphere, the sea.

Living silver
tumbles
into the dark
hold at slithery harvest.

So much
death and life
at once it makes
the head spin, lightly
like the double-talk
of oracles, or the sting
and flutter of the bouzouki
at night, in the tavernas
where something fresh
out of time comes back
to dance inside them.

4

Childhood, late-summer morning, hot
sun on my face. From far away
the sound of the sea
breeze, crisp in papery reeds
that bend, gently
under the sweet heft of tassels,
and there's that smell:
brackish water, creosote and fish.

When I break through the curtain
of tall stems, the jar of water
glitters with prismatic light
and a sense of freedom
sings like line from the reel of locusts.

I kneel on the bank
crumbling soda crackers
into a pocket of window screen
stapled at the end of a long stick
and lower it, slowly, into black
scum. Taut wrist
muscles ache and itch
under maddening beads of sweat
but I know they're there, thick
as my thumb, dim green …

NOW!

I lift it like a flag and watch
a sack of sleepy water
gush and leave
them skittering
in the light
screen
until they wear
themselves out, and lie
twitching, their bellies flashing
absolute silver through pulp and sea moss.

Glassed in, they idle
their fins (thin-ribbed
plasma fans) or snap
their dreamily lax
tails into a glide.

Their button eyes reflect
nothing. After a while
I'll carry them home
and feed them till they die.

5

Out of the surf's curl and collapsing rush
a mist opens and rides downwind, burned
in a brief rainbow. I cast as far as I can
and let the undertow take the lure
deep. There's a nick
and a tug and I lift the tip
of the rod and it bends and line speeds
from the reel's blurred spindle
with a metallic skirl then slows
as the channel purls and explodes.

The steelhead stands
on his tail, shakes, and falls
back, dives, and runs, and runs
again, till he comes up and floats
on his side, gill-covers opening
over crimson frills,
the rest of him shimmering
with prismatic echos in the late light ...

6

The overcast thins, brightens, and flowers

I don't know the names of give stray petals up to the freshening breeze,
a migration of butterflies from the esplanade's wood planters down to the sea.

Out on the water, a small boat is chasing a flock of gulls.
They rise and swirl into broken fingerprints,
barking, scolding, settling farther away.

A teenage waitress sweeps around chair legs and under tables
on the deck of a seafood restaurant, collecting dust,
wrappers and cigarette butts into small piles.
When she goes inside for a moment, the wind scatters them.

Sunday. A day without shadows. On Water Street, the gift
shops are open but the bars are closed. Strollers
breathe deeply and stop to scan the harbour
where the tall-masted boats rock at anchor
and the tide climbs a slope of darkened stones.

Then someone points, cries out. Just beyond
where the cove opens into the Bay of Fundy,
parting a white veil of mist that clings to the sea,
something sleek and slow and huge rises, blows, glides
by like a dream and its one fin lifts, arcs, then slips
back under silvery swells, and even those who have not

seen it murmur, as they collect along whatever edge the sea
affords, and squint through the suddenly magical
haze, more awake than they ever thought they'd be
on a morning like this, when nothing much is supposed
to happen, a day of rest, but a day of wonder too, and before long
the great finback and her calf come up again, crease the soft
plane of the shifting, nearly flat, rolling field of the bay, one plume

then another, and we can hear it, a burst
hiss, miraculous and common as the cracked tab
of a beer or a soft drink but so much more
complex though it's only water mixed with breath
and blown to mist by lungs the size of a bedroom,
and because they are rarely seen this close they are met
with stunned silence, and no one tries to fix this
apparition on film but we feel the weight, the gravity,

of each other's presence, miles and miles along the shore,
and for a brief time we understand, without anxiety,
how immense it is, how old, this gathering at land's end,
this kindred-visit out of the deep, so fabulous
-ly other, but known to us because we breathe the same air,
drink from the same source at birth, breed and fade in the same
shallow light, here, where we love what the sea provides ...
beautiful vistas, difficult work ... and all it saves us from
drowning in – our own blind wish for windfall or godsend.

# Road to the Sky

### 1

The first gold was morning
                       light in clear water
or early evening dusting the backs of sheep.
Now light cuts
            tiny diamonds
from a glass paperweight.
                  Time
travels at different speeds: Consider
the edge of a glacier, the heartbeat of small animals ...

### 2

When I was a child, before
I understood physics, I loved
the way a spoked wheel could turn
so fast it threw off a ghost
of itself that spun backwards
and this became a proof
of everything I wanted to believe in,
synchronicity, optics, my immortal soul.

3

The overcast breaks up and sunlight spills
                                    into the street.
Between backlit tenements, a flare of gold, a promise,
burns, chaotic but pure, beyond the last wrought-iron fence.

Once, in Rome, I watched a fountain gather the shades
                    and values
of a Tintoretto dusk into gorgeous foam, a moment so
                    full it felt
as though my life had completed itself.

                                    Thinking of that
            moment
I want to drive all night, I want to be ragged, unshaven,
            hungry and lost
in the dawn, I want to believe
that beauty still has the power to change us.


4

The land is so flat, any road I take leads to the sky,

and something is always going on there,
the flicker and smoke of tall storms,
flotillas, approaching or dwindling away,
polished rails that fuse at the vanishing point,
the glass dance of heat waves,
ember gardens, then
over the swift river of atmospheres
and the landscape's blackening map
the precise crawl of a star clock.

5

Frequency drift.
A country music station comes on strong.
Then crooked light-roots crack the dark
and static breaks out like a rash
of mosquito kamikazes
sizzling among the guitars and voices.

*Once, in the mountains,*
*I passed a valley of silk*
*haze printed with birds.*

Now the Milky Way spins a mist
beyond the moon, a violence
of disintegrating lights
like whipped intelligence ...

Up ahead there's a wash
of effervescence. A city ...
No, it's a drizzle
                    of fireflies.

The windshield fills with eerie wreckage
and as its luminescence fades
tranquil blinks condense
to a scar in the rear-view mirror.

6

How did I make my way across that waste
             of sand
                    and wind?
After what seemed like months of blind tunnelling,
there was an outcrop of smooth stone, thistles,
a field of wheat. *Welcome*
*to the Sunset Motel* (faded neon)
and a string of weathered shacks above the sea.

7

Plugged cannons in the rain
                         aimed at an empty bay.
Statues and memorial plaques flake in the weather.

Set in a low hill, the door
of a powder magazine's windowless room
stands open. It became too damp
for ammo, but found good use
as a prison.

            The high, clear
voice of a child pretends
to scold her brother.
                    'Get down
in the dungeon, you been bad!'
                         But he won't
so she harries him, in
                    and out
of the jail's thick skull, skidding
over wet grass, laughing
and I wonder if she knows she's laughing
at the grim remains of history in this place ...

8

It feels as though the road goes on forever.

Up ahead, men work. Cutting brush. Burning.

Above them, a drift of Autumn clouds.
How I love those soft shadings,
blue-white, grey, lavender, beige ...
There is something there, of comfort, of sustenance,
but something, too, of time
passing.
          On the river, a skiff
grows smaller and smaller until it gets lost in the waves.


9

A corridor of white
                    light through the pines. I remember
the blast of a locomotive
                    headlight, panning
diamonds from the snow ... mirrors
and smoke: now is the instant flying.

10

Along a straight road, blond specks
accelerate to matchsticks,
                              to telephone poles
peeled and fresh in a rush of wind. It's almost
dangerous
            the way the world speeds by,
                                          around
and beneath me, as though I were skimming
page after page for the one
                        sentence
                                  I've quoted
a thousand times, but have forgotten.

                * * *

Suddenly, for no reason I can see,
                            there is a burst of black
birds over the trees (bees from a scorched hive, bits
of charred paper)
                swirling
                        around some inscrutable threat.

                * * *

Listening to the wind
rush by an open window,
the static of tires on wet pavement, music
from the stereo, sleep
seeps in from the clouds
and I drift
        off
                into the sweetness
of my own melting
                heartbeat

that skips
        and rockets
as terror yanks me back …

        \* \* \*

              Because death is always
never more than a moment
                  away, we can't be free
of its weight
            or its pressure unless we absorb it
into our most intimate
               textures and calculations.

It is difficult, perhaps impossible, to think of this
without fear. And yet, sooner or later,
we will have to stare into the dark,
without blinking, without turning away.

What happens then is anyone's guess: emptiness, anger,
a great sadness crowned with splinters of joy …

        \* \* \*

Night. Storm clouds. Wind without rain.
The trees flutter their broken wings.
                Across black water
there is a window, a room filled with firelight and the shadows
of dancers that bend like flowers under the sea.
                   I'm learning
that solitude is a kind of presence, like the memory
of an animal I loved
            as a child
and could say anything to. Slowly, I'm discovering
that the future is not a result, or a place we must get to.

And what I see, in moments like these,
is how the self
       exults,
             in its own transparency, its flowing away.

     * * *

Sunday morning. Whitewashed walls. The hard, narrow bed. Bells
have a sacred cadence in this light. My breath
steams over coffee. Soon I will drive through the city
and out past the canal, where willows let their yellow-green rain
down into still reflection. A glass world where nothing moves.

The descent into emptiness is without conflict, without resistance.
The road opens again beside wide water,
                 adagios of islands and clouds.

11

On the rolling prairie, ploughed fields
are brown corduroy worn to beige at the crests
of hills where the wind has dried them. And now
a cloud spreads from the edge of the sky
like dark smoke, or the ink
                          of a cuttlefish.
When the rain comes
it smells like the windowsills of abandoned farms.

          * * *

The windshield is smothered
with mist, and hail; the sky,
the Trans-Canada, erased by grey
                          fury, then
the press of heavy weather spins
                          off,
and the road, the grass
                  shoulders are littered
with seed
          pearls, and the valley, already
                          in shadow, blinks
with the scattered attractions of Saturday Night.

12

Light lingers
           over the darkening hills
                      like an echo.
Looking out
           past the blue tablecloth, the flatware
with its constellation of silver
                  highlights,
through cold glass at the top of a Holiday Inn, I think,
*I could live the rest of my life in this place,*
drinking in the horizon's burnt gold
through a windbreak of wolf willows,
watching smoke rise from the chimneys,
blown leaves in the streets, and by the time
food arrives the sky is lit like a harbour.

In the window, the face
that smiles back at me is my own.


13


Summer's gone. Houses pass in the dusk.
A glass left out on the arm of a deck chair
gleams, nearly filled with forgotten rain. Miles
and miles of orchards. Lamps flare in the wind
sending flurries of warm light into branches
that bend with the weight of ripening fruit.
I drive all night under wet stars, cold
then nearly frozen
                  air, pouring
                          through the window, singing
songs I thought I'd left in another life.

14

The sun resides in everything under the sun:
leaves that glow like paper lanterns,
air in my lungs oxidizing minute brilliance,
insect wings, the eyes of small animals:
light of the mind and light of the world
at once, in which the colours and densities
of surfaces dissolve
                         to luminous marrow,
                                        burning
through every form in the visible world.


15

Clouds again. The high frontier
of daydream: puffed
agate
        cliffs, groves
of coral, outbacks and lit
interiors ... *go ahead*
*invent a tissue of white lies.*

In these gauze mansions ...
Beyond the savannahs of white grass ...
Whenever children of the moon ...

*No. What would you wish*
*on a star for?*

## 16

To stand at the end of the road's reason for going
on through shadows and broken codes, undistracted
by glimpses or hearsay, surrounded, again,
by everyday light, and a past which is not history.

From here, time elaborates consequence.
In the old market square, a fountain's rusted
mouth brims, runs. Woodsmoke and rain.
A touch of frost. A season of charms and risk.

# Dancing, with Mirrors

It's what she does to keep
her dream self apart
from critical paths, paper

clips, charts
and performance appraisals.
After work, in the dark

she begins: *battement, arabesque, fouetté
en tournant* ... to applause her heart
can rise from, though she knows her play

ballet won't change the way her grown
friends keep slipping away
into marriages, or solitudes of their own.

*Alone:* a relentless bell, the scrape
of teacup on saucer, rooftop sunsets, stone
-ware and magazine photographs taped

to the wall: rainbow decals: tricks
of light: letters: houseplants: drapes:
then a weekend of concerts and casual sex.

2

Morning. Annette's gone
                    downhill
over the slate-
                    green river
to work. I sit in the cold
kitchen, watching her things, the remains
of breakfast, a sheer blouse draped over a chair,
light through a blue bottle, burning
a vivid stain into the Irish wool
of my sweater.
                    In the window
a crystal turns on a string
and its blurred rainbow
drifts like a lost feather across the floor.
I feel her absence close
around me, draining the room to shades
of grey. I force the stuck door
to the roof with my shoulder,
and step out onto the snow's blank page.

A jet climbs over the city.
Its vapour trail fades into blue
distance. The air
sparkles with minute flakes
and sunlight is a faint astringent,
rinsing my fingers as they pull apart
stale toast for the sparrows.

How quickly they arrive,
fluffed by the wind, cheerful
and quarrelsome. They pick
the white silence clean and leave
an illegible memo, footprints
like a barbed-wire shadow
scrawled in the snow.

3

*Drunk shouts from the street melt*
*into sleep, and the dim, sleek*
*shapes cruise and cruise and strike*
*and she kicks back through the bell*
*-buoy heart's red wash and* breaks
out of breath, into dust,
into a clutter of old clothes,
old books. Slowly
she begins to trust
her ears: the ticking
snow, far-off, echo-y
tires on wet streets, the sadness
of time. And there's no one to kiss
her to sleep again, so she hugs
her pillow hard to the hollow
undertow that aches and leaves
her weak, knees
to her chin, her eyes
pinched against the spurs
of light that have already started
to flare in around her
Japanese window shade.
Sparrows accelerate
their helter-skelter chatter,
and voices from the next
apartment seem to exhale
the analeptic fragrance
of coffee.
From a snug wrap
of cottons and body heat she slides
into the chill, raises the shade, leaps

across the oak floor and spins
to a rush of wind through leaves and ferns
at the edge of a lake while thin

flurries ignite in the sun and burn
the city behind her. Her skin
breathes and glows. She turns

everything off but the silver world
of blocked and reversed light
where the long rope of her hair, her curved

arms, nearly girlish breasts and smooth
legs race with a snowstorm. Flakes
collect on the roof. Soon

she will have to choose
a disguise for the workplace.
One last kick and she comes to rest, ties

her hair in a loose knot,
pulls a denim skirt over her thighs.
Blouse. Knee socks. Hiking boots.

Down the street and across the bridge,
her heart adjusts to the throb
of stuck traffic, but beautiful moves

inside her winter coat keep
her easy and warm
and a thousand miles away

I remember her grey-green eyes,
how they dawned under cover
of dusk in the park, when she teased

her blue kite from the shadows
of trees, higher
                    and higher,
a wanderer tuned by love to the changing sky.


4


High water never lasts.
And when it's gone, bones
bleach in the sun.

For weeks her face will float into my mind
like music from a campfire down on the beach.
It's lovely, but it worries me,

this early symptom of Romance
which I distrust. We are not those glowing examples
concocted and improved upon for years

by movies and magazines and how-to books.
I was twenty-two when she was born
and I've already failed at most of what she believes in.

5

Behind me, distorted megaphone voices fade
as I reach the small cave between two hills.
Inside, there's blue light and a trail that pulls
and pulls. It's covered with loose rock and the grade
is steep but I climb up towards a sound that spills
over my skin like a harp's bright cascade.
Slow waves begin in my shoulder blades
and press through me. First fever, then chills
until I step out into a bright landscape:
lawns, a still pond, a stack of books
and a dancer wrapped in green wind. She looks
like the future, smiling; but blinks when I take
a page from each leather-bound volume – strokes
of an axe deeper than history – and fold paper
boats that drift in the soft breeze I make
with my breath. A mast begins to sprout, then streaks
up as the pond grows wide as a lake.
I leave my feet and splash into the sky.
It's cool, and warm, and smells like mown grass.
When I climb on deck, she's already there, shy
but flushed, and firm as a promise. I want to kiss
her mind, her flickering eyes. She tilts her head,
our bodies close, but before we touch I'm awake
in the cold, in the dark, and alone in bed.

6

The stained-glass hurricane lamp
changes her attic room
to a tent of lucid wings that breathe.

We lie in the bath, touching
until what we feel rising
is shocked by porcelain
and we drop back into small talk,
our stomachs fluttering
like the thin flame
that sends waves of tinted gloss
over her collarbones
and I can feel years of darkness
dissolve under her hands
as we pause between flights,
half in
          half out of the water.

7

Caught in a late-spring storm
I hardly know what I feel and
I can see those words *delight*
and *failure* lift like aimless
wings from this memory I have
of absolute piano the violins
the birch fire flaming up and
the intimate soft but now and
then awkward moves we forgave
our muscles for so completely
there because we did not want
to let the days and nights of
privacy build their invisible
walls between us for a second
longer and we have never been
closer or more beautiful slap-
happy as kids discovering new
ways to please each other and
the shadows ate us and we ate
the light that flamed over us
and in our eyes even the slip
of a tongue or elbow did not
spoil the rush of the moment
but now in the chillout of a
white freeze-frame I scratch
ice from the car windows and
close my cumbersome hangover
around this unwiltable image
I keep of us inside the fire
light and the music and that
starry promise disintegrates
in a biting wind salted with
tiny diamonds and a headache

begins to pull its conundrum
tight around this cold fever
because I take her more than
I want to inside my personal
sense of doom like a blossom
I need to ignore because the
only language I know has not
said the words she hoped for


8


Tall rocks chew the sky.
Flax floats in its own blue mist.

*Brat of my dreams, I wilt*
*for the brush of your careless fingers,*
*the jade smoke of your eyes.*

9

This time, when we take off
our clothes, there's a different
energy; her skin's flushed, her breath
quick and shallow. I know
she's met someone. I like the strangeness
and her appetite for sex, but after
she tells me, she's upset because I'm not.

*Does this mean our romance
has entered a terminal coma?*

Later, we kiss goodbye
under breezy novocaine music
and I walk back past the waiting
room's black, Naugahyde chairs,
through a glass corridor
down a flight of steel stairs

and out into the cold dusk
where miles of street lights
like bronze and silver pins
burn through blue shadows.

When I get home, the lights are still on.
She's left a pair of thin corduroy slacks
like a shed skin on the carpet.

By now she is in bed
with a stranger who drinks
what I still think of
as the deep-sea light of her eyes.

I listen to late jazz and imagine
different futures, wriggling
into death like fish on a dock.
I search my cargo of darkness
but nothing wrestles there;
those jealous flares
that would pit my music against his Porsche
have burned out long ago …

Then the phone rings.

He couldn't stay
the night and she's feeling …
restless. Her throaty laugh
reminds me of Saskatoon,
how we woke and made love in the dark,
then drifted back into still-warm dreams,
how we wanted each other
again after breakfast in bed,
after old photographs,
after chocolate and Japanese apple pears
all afternoon in the dead of winter

     *sex is a language, not an event*

and before long we find ourselves
remembering how we slogged
across town through snow in a freezing wind
to sit in the last row (her frostbitten toes
in my fleeced boots, my feet in her hat
on the floor) of that shabby theatre
where we held each other and couldn't let go
through both showings of *Dr. Zhivago*.

10

The moon is up. The park is empty.
I stand on the wooden bridge, listening
to cables vibrate in the soft gale
that lapses and gusts, sultry, then cool,
but dense with the scents of summer,
a breath of air so fresh it melts
the heaviness of absence, of time,
and it feels good to be on my own
again, watching the river's lustre
curve away into black trees.


11


Coming in from the channel
under clouds with fiery skirts,
the wind easy, the bow of the ship
hissing through soft swells,
the engine humming, the harbour
aglow in the deepening shadow
of mountains, I stand at the rail
and watch a handful of fool's gold
grow, slowly, disclosing
its tiered streets and lit windows.

I cross the gangplank
over the slap of black water
and make my way uphill
through shouts and scraps of music
toward the tables of a small café
thinking of her, remembering
nights I scanned the horizon,
how her eyes returned
and flickered like uncertain stars.

12

We saved up time, five days
for this cabin off in the bush.

We burrow under the quilt,
between cold sheets,
our bodies barely touching.

We are careful. We kiss
for a while with our eyes
                    open,
then read our magazines in buttery light
until the glossy pages slip from her fingers
and she rests her head against my shoulder.

I remember how her eyes glowed
through the smoke of hospitality rooms,
the way her toes curled in their socks
under the table before her feet,
like small animals, climbed into my lap
while her voice went on with a story …

Something collects inside me, as though
my whole past were present at once,
and I feel it leap like a sinew of sweet light
into her sleep.
                    She shivers and moves closer.

13

Evenings, we light candles,
heat water on the black wood stove.

Slippery in a tin tub, we gossip and joke
watching our shadows loom and shrink on the wall.

Through the long afternoons
we discover the luxuries of silence.

On our last night, we watch the moon
scattering petals across the lake.

A cold wind pours, and sputters.
She pulls my arms around her shoulders,

warming us both. In the distance
a star trembles; waves crash on the rocks.

Is this really it? she asks, her voice
like water, clear, and strong,

and without having to think,
I answer yes, it is.

14

She stacks the glasses upside down
on the wrong shelf, borrows my things
without asking and forgets
where they are.
                    I wear my shoes
in the house, drink milk straight
from the carton, sleep
late and work all night.

We quarrel over these
behaviours, but what remains
between us is the gap
of years, my need
                    for solitude,
her lifelong friend's three kids.

15

*Let's go someplace*
*where the breeze is always*
*fresh and cool in the sun.*

I'm reading her note, signed
*love,* on the patio at my regular
bar. I turn in my chair
and the frame grates on rain-pocked cement.

Above the burned-out lawn, grackles
veer and swoop like an obsolete air show.
A rude wind scatters papers
from this tabletop *in the sun*
and already the light has taken me
back to that beach where a breeze from the sea
would scatter the shadows of her hair
over crossword puzzles all afternoon
and long-legged birds would come down from the sky
to walk on wet sand, so awkwardly,
their crooked feet printing intricate codes
where the waves turned over, and spread
their temporary mirrors *in the sun.*

*Let's go someplace where the breeze comes up off the water,*
*where the nights are soft and deep and full of stars.*
*Let's walk through the empty streets of old stone cities,*
*and out along a curved blade of sand, revived*
*by the suddenly cold air and the sound*
*of breakers toppling and hissing*
*paving the beach with marble*
*foam in the moonlight ...*

Last week we sat and smoked in a thunderstorm
on the cedar deck behind our house, till we were
transported, by laughter, and blue light, and rain.


16


A child begins to appear in her dreams.
A boy child, night after night.

Sometimes she wakes up grieving.
She's lost him, he's wandered off
at a bus station, a forced-labour camp.
Or he crawls across the soft dunes
and arroyos in the palm of her hand,
his cries sharp, and small, and far away.

I feel her longing. I dream about him too.

17

I wake in the dark and slip out of bed,
listening to hear if I've changed
her breathing. Her face on the pillow
is beautiful, the way a moonlit reflection
on water is, and I remember how she sank
into sleep, her head on my shoulder
that first night in our wilderness
cabin, how she was there,
and not there,
                    like the shadow of a bird,
alighting
        in the shadow of a tree.

18

Why do I still think of her voice
as an angel trapped in the soft rain of the shower?

I sit at the window, more and more closed
in the silence that jelled after she left
for work. The furnace clicks
and expires; air vents tick, the electric
clock whines like a stuck mosquito.

There are always risks. In love
even success can be stifling, like too much
ease. Soon we will drift close again,
get caught up and lost
as if in the pleasures of a magnetic storm,
but for now there is this tough stretch
of patience: winter outside, the apple tree
stranded in deep snow, arthritic
twigs knotted against the glare, its trunk
mottled, like a thousand-year-old egg.

　　　　　* * *

The cider's not ready to bottle yet.
It stands in a glass carboy, breathing
while gravity settles the haze
of its mild but transformational
ferment.
　　　　　I see myself
in the highest branches, reaching
for half-rotten fruit, tossing them into a basket
or shaking the tree so crabs will rain
down on the beautiful groundling
who gathers them up
and yells at me with her tangy voice
because I neglected to warn her

before I became a two-fisted storm in the boughs.
And suddenly I'm surrounded
by yellow jackets. They buzz my ears
and tumble over my fingers, nipping
at brown pulp and rising heavily into the air.

Once, when I was a boy,
they attacked and left me blind
for days, but now their bumpy flights
are openly disorganized
and it's clear these childhood terrors
(helter-skelter war parties
gone astray in my hair
or stumbling over the nap of my flannel shirt)
have imbibed the spirits of wild yeast
and surprise themselves by melting
into fits of laughter I can't hear.

19

Through a screen dusted with inside light
above clay pots of thyme and coriander and sorrel
the front hedge is an inkblot, an absence
(except when cars pass on the street, scattering
red and white and amber
fireflies through dense leaves).
Beyond it the neighbourhood sleeps.

In front of the pink bungalow, backlit
by a high globe in the alley, a fir
sags, shaggy and black as a wilderness
exile. Behind it, to the left,
a loose cliff of softwood leaves that hiss
in the breeze, washed by the same light
that soaks into brick and fills the eaves
of a dormer with shadow dust.

Brisk air cools the sunburned skin
under my eyes. It carries the thin harmonics
of night birds and far-off traffic,
odours of wet grass, exhaust fumes
and cedar from a rain-soaked deck. Sometimes
a motorcycle starting up, or a voice,
or a rash of voices, or a scrap
of music from a car window stirs
the silence. Sometimes a jet
sails its cluster of lights over the trees
and now a siren stretches thin and breaks
into quick echoes, then fades and revives and fades
into the diesel blast of a train
at a crossing, but mostly it's quiet.

Split, stacked birch against the wall,
the ripple patterns of light through rattan
lampshades on the ceiling, and the geraniums
blooming on leggy stems in their rough peat pots
compose the kind of sweetness travellers catch
a glimpse of as they pass in the night
and maybe wistfully long for. What do I long for
beyond this comfortable house I've wrapped myself up in
as though it could protect me from the dark?

On the scarred oak
table Annette began to strip last fall,
a cheap straw hat I bought on the road
the year I went home to help my mother
die, stands in the soft light, its crown
splintered, its brim stained with sweat.

I promised not to miss her, but I do.

20

I pick her up at the airport and she drives
home through the winter dusk, chatting
happily about her trip, our friends
in Toronto, wanting to know
if I've kept the house neat and washed
yesterday's dishes, my hands, my clothes.

I've cooked a soup of squash,
caramelized onions, carrots
and baby shrimp, a first
course before the marlin
and asparagus we feed each other
on the rug before a birch fire.

We leave the dishes
and climb to the top of the house
where she lights scented candles. We kiss
and hold each other a long time
before we undress
and slip under cool sheets. When I reach
to open the drawer of the nightstand
she says, 'It's my safe time,
I don't think we need
protection.'

*Protection.* The word
reminds me that I'm still afraid
of what we both want, this child
who comes to us then disappears
from our dreams. Do I really
(will I ever) have enough
love, patience, money? Can *we*
rethink ourselves, fight
off our minor demons, carry
a new life between us
and keep it safe, and keep it strong?

21

Eight weeks and there's no blood.
She's been upstairs with a kit
from the drugstore, and her face
is pale but intense as she climbs
over my chest and squeezes in
on the wrong side of the bed, staring
up through the ceiling.

It was blue, she says. Blue.

I stare up too, as though
some version of the future might appear
there, by accident or by design,
but all I see is the same old
cracks
          and shadows.
                          I don't know
what to say. We hold hands
and watch the day go on
without us. We need to take
this in, but there's no time. Tomorrow
we leave with friends for Thailand.

22

In the great temple at Chiang Mai
it is Sunday. Annette draws the teak log

back, then releases it.
A low musical shock wave

changes the light around our bodies,
hums through marrow and bone.

He could feel that, she says, partly
to me, but mostly to the world

at large, and I don't want to move
away from this moment, this

clarity at the centre of change.

23

Koh Samui. On our way
to the restaurant, she stops
to watch a toddler, who sits
on her heels, reaching
for a beach ball that floats
in the pool beyond her
stretched fingers. A breeze
comes up and skims it along
the tiled edge. The child
stands up and teeters after it,
holds out a hand, as though
offering tidbits to a pet.

After we're seated, I notice
that Annette's not listening
to John read the menu,
and she keeps glancing
past me, back towards the pool.
She asks, 'Is anyone watching
that child?' and as we look
around for the waiter she
bolts from her chair, hurdles
the low hedge just in time
to lift a bewildered
moppet out of the drink.

Later she explains, 'The ball
blew away from the edge
and the girl stepped out
as though she could walk on water.'

24

Back in Canada I've got high fever,
vertigo, chills. I take malaria pills

but it's just a bad case
of the flu. By the time I can stand

again she's brought home
a book of names. At the hospital,

ultrasound
looks like the pygmy black-and-white

set that let me escape
into old films in the dream life

I lived before this one
woke me. It's fuzzy

with echoes that explode
like snow in a dark wind.

But someone's there, a smudge
of light with a pulse,

a hundred beats a minute,
then a flash and the blurred sweep of an arc,

left leg back over his head
like the great Pele, or a dancer at night in the park.

25

Beauty is not a stable
characteristic. It flares
and passes. Often
when she is not aware of it
her face releases itself to a small,
pure event, and her whole life
is that moment, peeling a grape,
pruning the tip of a houseplant,
measuring water into a glass cup.


26

At the doctor's, I can't believe
that I feel proud, as though
I'd invented her buoyancy,
her sexy heft onto the table.

Brian squeezes gel from a tube
onto her taut skin, slides
the black disk around till he finds
what he's after, then he turns up

the gain. It sounds
powerful and otherworldly,
like a shadowy but irresistible force
that has always been there, deep, in the sea.

In the early dusk, we kiss, lightly,
and walk to our cars. We could be seen
as figures in some tragic tale, and I feel
this odd rush of pleasure because we're not.

27

We lie in the dark, listening
to *Classics of the Baroque*. Night
unfolds like a complex flower
and I can hear her throat
open. She's whispering. 'He's awake.
It feels like fins in water.' And before
I can answer she goes on. 'Shhh ... it's
changing. There. He's got it.'

And when I lay my palm on her tight flesh
I can feel his kicks, an exact beat
keeping time with Albinoni.

28

Transition.
When the waters broke she felt
his terror. Now, in the half
sleep between contractions
she opens her eyes. Their grey-
green light draws me in
as she hums and hums like a perfect
animal.

          Hours
have no meaning. When I look
up, the clock has skipped
half a day, half a night.

Then I'm standing with the doctor
leaning into the push of her foot,
her leg, her scent, her effort.
He's almost here. The crown
of his overlapped head plates presses
and recedes. Her lips are a door, a gate.

The needle goes in, comes out.
There's a thin spurt of blood.

Then the knife. But the muscle
holds. One more push. One more. One more.
And the head comes through.
Brian turns him. His face
is the face of a Mayan courier
who has run hundreds of miles without sleep.
His baby chest heaves
in, heaves, he's
blue. He can't
breathe.

Then the thick-veined
cord, beautiful as a coil of wet
marble bleeds, pulls away and he's gone
from us. I can hear suction
tubes and a loud cry, then I'm rising
through bright floors and wards and landings
until I'm standing beside his house
of glass, flooded
with oxygen. There's nothing
I can do while they X-ray his lungs.

He has big hands, a round
face, he is here, he is brave, he is not
afraid, I think he knows
that those tall creatures
hovering above him like white birds
of prey are there
to help him.
   Later, from a wheelchair,
she reaches in and his fist closes around her finger.

  *Love is a mirror*
  *in which we learn to dance.*

# A New Life

### 1

He's never done this before,
but his lips take the rubber nipple
and work it hard, dragging
sugar water from a world he never dreamed
existed, strange to him
as it must have been to the first life
that crawled from the sea into unbreathable air.

When the bottle's nearly drained
his eyes close and he's asleep
in my arms, in a room filled with sterilized light.

### 2

Inch by inch, it disappears, crackling
into my fist and he screams
with delight, pulls it straight, a snake
of wrinkled, glassy light, then lets it lie
rustling, and watches with a cat's attention
as the cellophane tube shrinks again
into my working fingers. This
goes on for what seems like hours and he
is never bored, his whole body tense
with expectation, his six-month mind,
endlessly,
        hungry for the same
               surprise.

3

He has crawled under a dresser
in the bedroom and won't come out.
We stare at each other across
this impasse, and suddenly, without
thinking, we both begin
to laugh, as though we have seen,
at the same time, the beautiful
absurdity of our world.

4

The days have settled
into spontaneous
routines. After his nap,
he doesn't cry to be picked up
but lies there practising
random sounds that will evolve
into syllables, then words.

On the change table, he kicks
and smiles, happy to be free
of clothes for a while, and his eyes
brighten as I bundle him up
in his blanket, his zipper bag,
and strap him onto my back.

Off we go into the white
afternoon, all the way
to the letter box and back,
his voice a cheerful
palaver over my shoulder
and when I tell him, look
at the snow, Evan, he answers,
'no! 'no! Then laughs,
as though that was
the funniest word in the world.

5

A spray of white
stars and a sickle
moon on the blue

shade, lit
from inside. I sit
in the car, listening

to news: of the war, shells
blowing up taxis and hospitals, news:
of a sniper, loose on the freeway,

suicide bombers, guns
in the schools. He's
asleep in his crib,

no blanket, his legs tucked
under his chest, shadow bars
like prison stripes across

his back. I remember
rocking him in the soft light
before nightfall, the comfort

of his weight, and the way
he takes my glasses
off, carefully

folds them
and hands them
back, like a cancelled weapon.

6

I've fed him and he's happily stuffed
into his chair. I go to the sink
to rinse his bowl and flatware.

When I turn to check it's already
too late. He's climbed up
and out, he's left
his balance point and he's
toppling but acrobatically
twists in the air
and smacks the floor with his back.

I'm frozen, shocked. I expect
him to scream but he doesn't, he just
lies there and blinks, limp as a rag
doll, and I'm down
                              on my knees, foolishly
asking 'Are you all right?' I don't
know what to do, or if I should
touch him or how
                              to help and I reach
carefully under his legs, his back,
lift him and carry him ten long miles
to the living room where I sink
into the couch.
                              He has disappeared
into himself and I think
of Annette, how she gathered
herself into the same absolute
acceptance, her animal
distance minding the pain
of his birth, and I can't
believe how stupid, how careless

I've been. I have this thought,
rewind the tape, revise
this narrative because it's not
right, and the helpless
futility of that
idea
    breaks
in my throat, a rough
grunt as he begins to
breathe, hard, like the way he fought
for air in those first moments
away from the dark, the beautiful warmth
of her body, and a weight
uncoils from my chest, he's not
going to die but his brain, his spine, what
about that, what broken
                future awaits him?
Then his eyes, the colour of river water,
change from silty to translucent
amber. He burps, kicks,
wiggles and I know
how it must feel to be plucked
back from the deep
circles of Dante's Hell.

7

He's a toddler now.
I've built a portable platform
for him to stand on and look out
through any window in the house.

He's learned to say
goodbye with a wave.
And he knows the word
for his mother's red Scirocco.

A minivan drives by in the back lane.
He brightens. And as it disappears
from view, his arm goes up.
'Bye bye car car.' His first
sentence, already resigned
to transience and loss,
to the brevity of unexpected joys.


8

We take him to visit friends and he
disappears
                    into a room where the stereo
shakes, pours out
                    salsa
                              and that's where we find him,
his eyes glowing and focused
                              but lost
to everything in the world except what comes up
through the floor and in through his ears,
                                        driving
his legs to a standing sprint,
his arms taut with the stretch and lift of wings.

9

We're taking our time
on a hiking trail around Inverness Falls
when we notice he is no longer
with us.
            Far away, very small under the trees,
he gives himself up to that now-familiar
seizure. We can't
figure out what brought this on,
but slowly, under the birdcalls,
the scurry of small animals,
the rush of wind through aspen leaves,
we hear what he's dancing to, maybe
the oldest voice on earth, water
pouring down from a drop fault
and foaming over the stones.

10

Christmas in Mexico. At the Posada
Tiburon, he ventures
a little way from us to explore
the beach, walks cautiously up to the breakers,
talks to them then turns and runs
back, laughing. When he returns
to the table his eyes are bright, but he doesn't
speak, instead he gathers taco chips
and a piece of lime which he carries
and lays carefully at the edge
where the sand has begun to lose
its sheen. He waits for the next
wave to curl and when it gathers
his offering in its rush, he claps
and shouts, then performs
this ritual again, many times
before he sits down to dinner.

11

We're on a blanket
under the palm-frond shade
of Carrizalillo beach.

He takes a sip
from the coconut's candy-
striped straw, then spits it out.

An acquired taste
I think as I take it back
and suck down the cool sweet milk.

By nine p.m. and for three days
I'm in bed with a raging fever.

Annette thinks our son has a gift,
and perhaps a career
as a taster for celebs on world tours.


12


He floats around the pool
on a green, inflatable dinosaur, peering
at the tiny frogs that perch under the lip.

All at once he begins to declaim:
'Twas a Monday afternoon
on the twenty-third of June
when in Possum Creek a strange event occurred.'
And goes on to deliver,
perfectly, all seventeen stanzas
of *Possum One: The Outback Rocketship*.

13

Every afternoon before his nap
we lie in bed in the clean light
and I read him the same
adventure: Tigger as The Masked
Avenger, and his nemesis, El Conejo.

In the taxi, on our way
to the Airport in Huatulco
he starts to sing, four
notes – fifth, third and root,
root, in perfect pitch, El
Co-ne-jo, El Co-ne-jo,
over and over until the woman
we're sharing the cab with
twists around and asks
if we could please make him stop.


14

I take him for his afternoon walk
in the stroller. He is happy,
babytalking the birds, the squirrels.

My mind wanders, makes lists, calculates
income and expenses, and he begins
to whimper, to cry, to wail. How quickly
everything I thought so important
fades and there is only this
distress at his distress. When he feels
my attention surround him again,
his attention returns
to the autumn trees and the sky.

15

October, just after dark.
Evan is four, going on five.
We've been to the movie store and as we cruise
back toward the lit porch of our house, he says,
'It's a beautiful night, George, let's
just drive.' He adjusts
the radio to a quieter pitch,
and as we leave our neighbourhood
his eyes grow more intent, exploring
the soft night, the sudden vista when we cross
a bridge over water flecked with lights
and follow River Road to the edge
of the city. Through the open windows
a harvest-scented breeze, tinged with grass-
fire smoke, smells like a thousand miles
of prairie as cloud cover sails away
from the moon. A leaf comes loose
in the wind and scrapes across the windshield.
We seem to be gliding now, through a stillness
that is so clear it feels like time
has left the empty streets.

When I turn to see if he's ready
to start for home, he's leaning
back, his head cradled between the seat
and the door, asleep, and smiling.

16

The skis are short, and wide, and blue.

Half a mile into the cross-country trail
he falls, gets up, goes on, falls again.
Annette consoles him, 'Falling
is a part of skiing, Evan.' He thinks
about that, then shakes his head.
'Skiing is skiing and falling
is falling and I don't see
what's so skiing about falling.'

17

All morning I've felt cold static
creak in my ankle bones,
but it's my turn to tie skates
at the rink, at the school.

I'm late, but I've chosen this road
for the elms that close overhead
with a gesture I accept at once
as my own wish to shelter and protect.

Out on the ice, his puffed buff mittens
batter the air for balance, his body
takes the measure of time in a stretched
second. He turns, cuts
across his own undecipherable trail,
accelerates to the crisp edge
of wipeout. He knows
I'm there, in the stands,
unremarkable in my shabby coat,
and he carries this knowledge like a goblet
he will not drink himself, and will not spill.

18

At the airport in Winnipeg
I hug him and he stands back
next to his mother. His silence
is contemplative and I wish
I could hear what he's thinking.

It's never been so difficult
to leave before and I think
*I'll never be able to do this*
*again*, but then he smiles
and releases me
into a solitude that is immediate
and complete, the birthright
of consciousness, vacant only
in theory, entertained
by a long train of redeemed
failures, redundancies, a clearing
in the forest, a horizon
where something is always beginning
again, or sifting into disarray.

19

After twenty-six hours
without sleep, flying
effortlessly over three hundred million
lives, all that's left
is to drag my luggage up the stairs,
turn the key and enter
this white privacy, absence
in every room and the shock
of silence.
           Soon it will be dark.
There will be stars
and village lights
and their slick shimmer on the still sea.


20

Cool sheets. The body curls
around emptiness. Sleep
is a slow tide, a dangerous
helplessness the body needs
to heal. The mind splits,
and hums to itself as it enters
that memory of her voice in the rain.

21

Breaking up and floating – this
is the dream lapse and echo
that eases me back into time,
the spiral's heart, this intimate
suspension drenched
with the familiar
presence I understand
as my own when I return
through the star gate
where tomorrow becomes today.


22

The breeze is filled with distance
and thunder. Once, we sat on the deck
behind our house and smoked in the rain.

How long has it been, how much
has been forgotten, lost at sea, on the road,
in the sky between that moment and this

bristling scrap of daylight with its
pair of hawks, their cut shadows
skimming the brown grass.

23

*There*
>changes when I'm here, becomes
not only distant
>>but broken
into flashback episodes, highlights,
a drawer full of keepsakes and photos.

*I bundle him in the backpack*
*and set out into the winter*
*afternoon to mail my poems*
*off to a critical world. He points*
*at the white stuff in the trees,*
*in the bushes, and makes that*
*sound I love with his tongue,*
blabalabalabalabalablah. *I let him*
*out and he crawls into a drift,*
*picks it up, puts it in his mouth*
*and when it melts there is no end*
*to his wonder.*
>>I remember
how the world was once,
a place filled with miracles and games.

24

Morning. The sea is already
brisk, dotted with whitecaps.

Smoke from hundreds of cook fires
hangs like a blue mist,
over the beach, over the soft hills.

Something rises, a strong shift
in the wind, a spindrift
lit by rainbows from another
exile, frail as grace
or that moment before
dawn in which everything
is possible but not yet real.


25


Fishing boats that went out in the dark
return with their first catch, cut
their motors and slide, hissing
up on the sand. Snapper
and yellowtail and mahi mahi. Soon
the sound of butter foaming in the pan,
the fragrance of wild garlic, fish
flesh turning white, and the brown
-shelled, orange-yolked eggs of Mexico
will change this faraway workspace
into something a lot like home.

26

The beach at night is dangerous but irresistible,
zones of darkness and light, the Pacific
a shadowy presence, its crash and spray, distant
boat lights blinking like fat stars, and along the shore
the candles, the paper lanterns
of restaurants, the soft wash of guitars
and voices.
                    They are with me but far away.
I remember the week we spent here,
our dinner at the Posada Tiburon,
how Evan left his chair,
and ventured slowly across the sand
how he ran back from the toppling water,
and returned, time after time,
speaking in low tones,
as if to a large, unruly animal.

A waiter smiles, a child
sidles up to my table, she's
ten, maybe twelve, but small
for her age, wants to see
my journal, draws
awkward birds, a stick
priest and a clown, signs
laboriously, *Pilar
Veronica Cruz*, asks who *I* am,

where I came from, where my wife
might be tonight, and if my children love
to dance. She has seen me
here before and wonders,
why do I eat alone and why
do I stay so long when the meal
is done. For the lights,
I say, for the breeze, for the night
sky, and she looks out
at the sea, a child
scribbling in a notebook,
out after dark, on her own like me.

27

I came here to think, and to write.

It is the season of clouds, but not
yet the season of rain. Lots
of thunder and wet threat in the sky,
but the soft bricks and slick tiles are dry.

I want to see glass-bead curtains
blur the edges of all that is hard
and straight, I want to see lightning,
the *chubasco* crawling over the hills, spilling
its misty spritz onto the *playa central*,
where boys with stick legs
kick up gritty storms with a soccer ball.

What life can they expect
to flower out of this intermittent blaze
of sand, or the sea, the town
scattered like bright parcels
among the rocks that climb out of sight
where the coast range crests
into smoke trails and the drift of wings?

I wonder but will never know
what dreams they share, hunched
under thunderheads in the shadows of palms,
or gathered around the clear flame of a candle.

I ask myself,
What is this feeling
of being stuck for too long, halfway
between arriving and moving on,
and I think of my son, Evan, his voice
on the phone, very quiet.
*I have one question for you.*
    (pause)
*When are you coming home?*


28


Driven by cab across the bright night
city, listening to jazz, I remember:
this was the music of cigarette smoke, of desire,
for something I did not understand
back then, at loose ends
on the streets of New York, and it gave
the small hours a structure that hurt
less than the silence of time,
or the heartbeat of a nameless absence.

But tonight, the unpredictable idiom
of drum kit, sax, piano and bass
is softened *'round about midnight*
by the first creased leaves of spring
that pass overhead like a green mist
between the windshield and the racing moon,
and by the knowledge of where I'm going, home
to a sleeping house where my partner and our son
have just begun to improvise new dreams.

29

Today I'm a horse. Evan climbs on
and we gallumph a dozen times
around the track from the living room
through the hallway and back,
with appropriate neighs, rears
and sidesteps. Then he climbs off.
'Okay, you're George again. But
you must be thirsty, I'll get you a drink.'

The way he trots off
to the kitchen, I know he's up
to something. When he returns
I take a whiff. It's white
vinegar but I don't let on. 'Mmm,
filtered water, thanks.'
He looks disappointed, but
when I take a sip then spit it out,
he laughs and shouts.
'April Fool! April Fool!'
'But Evan, that was weeks ago.'
'I know, but you weren't here,
so I saved it for you.'

30

Hung from a branch, thin,
long-limbed, angular and slick
as glass, a creature with head spikes,
back spikes, elbow spikes, shines
in the winter sun and stares at the child
who stares back from the picture window
at the stringy fingers, the praying mantis head.

He recognizes the Ice Thing
from the movies he watches at night
in his dreams. A story begins
to unfold, how it hibernates in daylight,
then wakes and comes down to hunt
in the dark, how its bite will melt
small animals to plasma which it drinks
through a tube that sprouts from its chest.

He imagines adventures, crises,
how it stood once, frozen
in the headlights of a police cruiser,
then leapt, five or six times
its height to escape in the elms along the river.

All winter it hangs there, in the cold
light. Then, after a night full of rain,
it's gone. The child imagines it has returned
to the universe, galaxy, home world
or dimension from which it came; he listens
as it tries to explain, in that language
of hand signs, glottal clicks and sharp
harmonics, how it survived
separation from the collective
as none of its kind ever had, because
of a creature, an alien child
whose eyes glowed like the amber moons
above their white planet.

31

In the nearly wasted afterglow
of this cold summer's evening, I'm surrounded
by a thousand muted shades of green, and the cries
of seagulls blown down from the lake by the gathering storm.

It could be October except for the leaves
and the lingering light at ten o'clock. I wish
I could understand why I've been visited all afternoon
by so much happiness in so much gloom. Rain has begun

to dot the street and the walk. I can hear it ping
on the eavestroughs. The porch windows
are pearled with drops that collect and run
with candle flame on the glass. The light

is almost gone but the sky won't show
its hidden stars for an hour or more. I know
that my life is not what it might have been,
I could have done more, like you, or less;

come in from the wilderness of solo adventures
a lot sooner. But there is nothing in this pewter gleam
that troubles or confounds me. Soon, I will sleep.
Tomorrow, if it clears, I'll drink tea on the deck

then change into old clothes and top-dress the lawn.

# Acknowledgements

Parts of this poem have been published in the following books, anthologies, journals, magazines and periodicals, often in radically different versions. *Blood Ties* (Sono Nis Press, Vancouver, 1972), *Border Crossings, Canadian Literature, Contemporary Manitoba Writers* (Turnstone Press: Winnipeg, 1990), *Choice, CVII, Decal* (Wales), *Garden Varieties* (Cormorant Books, 1988), *Grain, The Globe and Mail, Harper's, Ideas of Shelter* (Turnstone, 1981), *Inscriptions* (Turnstone, 1993), *Italian-Canadian Voices* (Mosaic Press, Montreal, 1984), *The Literary Review of Canada, Margin* (England), *Matrix, The Moosehead Review, More Garden Varieties* (Aya Press, 1989), *Naugatuck River Review, New Mexico Quarterly, The New Quarterly, The New Yorker Book of Poems* (Viking: New York, 1970), *Nimrod, Open Country* (Turnstone, 1976), *Origins, Other Voices, Our Times, Out of Place: Stories and Poems* (Coteau Books, 1991), *The Pacific Quarterly Moana* (New Zealand), *The Penguin Book of Canadian Verse* (Hammondsworth, England; Markham, Canada; Victoria, Australia; New York; Penguin Books, 1975), *Poetry Canada Review, The Poets of Canada* (Hurtig,1973), *Prairie Fire, The Presence of Fire* (McClelland and Stewart, Toronto, 1982), *Prism International, Quarry, Relations* (Mosaic Press, 1986), *Rumours of Paradise/Rumours of War* (McClelland and Stewart, Toronto 1995), *Smatter o' Fact, Solstice 2, Sound Heritage, Sur* (Buenos Aires), *The Tamarack Review, Vintage 92: Prize Winning Poems from the League of Canadian Poets* (Sono Nis Press, 1993) and *Writers' News Manitoba.*

Section 18 of Canto III, 'What We Take with Us, Going Away', was first published in *The New Yorker.*

I am grateful to The Canada Council and The Manitoba Arts Council for grants which allowed me to work full time on this project. I would also like to thank Catherine Hunter, whose detailed response to a much earlier version changed its direction dramatically; Andy Patton for his numerous editorial queries and suggestions; Arlene Scully who rescued the first half of the book from a gaggle of missteps; Charles Wright, for his mastery of the long line, his generosity of spirit, his encouragement, his irresistible advice; Wayne Clifford for his testy insults; and Robin Hoople, whose immense learning, creative scholarship and articulate criticism brought the project into accurate focus.

# About the Poet

George Amabile has published his poetry, fiction and non-fiction in the USA, Canada, Europe, England, Wales, South America, Australia and New Zealand in over a hundred anthologies, magazines, journals and periodicals.

He was Writer-in-Residence at University of British Columbia for 1969–70, co-founder and editor of *The Far Point*, founder and editor of *Northern Light*, has edited a dozen titles for Nuage Editions, Signature Editions and Penguin, and has published eight books. From October 2000 to April 2001 he was Writer-in-Residence at the Winnipeg Public library.

*The Presence of Fire* (M&S, 1982) won the CAA National Prize for literature; his long poem *Durée* placed third in the CBC Literary Competition for 1991; 'Popular Crime' won first prize in the Sidney Booktown International Poetry Contest in February 2000; 'Road to the Sky' received a National Magazine Award honourable mention for 2000; 'What We Take with Us, Going Away' was shortlisted for the CBC Literary Prize in 2003 and he is the subject of a special issue of *Prairie Fire*, (Vol. 21, No. 1, May 2000). 'Diminuendo' was awarded third prize in the Petra Kenney International Poetry Competition for 2005 and 'A Raft of Lilies' won second place in the MAC national poetry contest, 'Friends' (2007). He has performed his poems on the CBC, at numerous venues in Canada and the USA, and at the Olympics in Montreal.

His most recent publications are *Tasting the Dark: New and Selected Poems* (The Muses Company, an imprint of Gordon J. Shillingford Publishing, 2001) and *Rumours of Paradise/Rumours of War* (M&S, 1995).